Brick

Monday morning in the *Brick* mailroom

Brick

a literary journal

number 69

spring 2002

PUBLISHER: Linda Spalding

EDITORS: Linda Spalding, Michael Ondaatje,
Michael Redhill, Esta Spalding
MANAGING EDITOR: Michael Redhill
DESIGN: Gordon Robertson
COVER AND GRAPHICS PRODUCTION: Rick/Simon
ASSISTANT EDITOR: Emmet Mellow
APOLOGIST: Cecily Moös

*Works of art are of an infinite loneliness and with
nothing to be so little appreciated as with criticism.
Only love can grasp and hold and fairly judge them.*
— Rainer Maria Rilke

ISSN 0382-8565
ISBN 0-9687555-3-4
Publications Mail Agreement # 1756346

We gratefully acknowledge the support of
The Canada Council and the Ontario Arts Council

Brick accepts unsolicited manuscripts of non-fiction *only*.
Please send submissions with appropriate return postage to:

BRICK
Box 537, Stn Q
Toronto, Ontario
M4T 2M5 Canada

Submissions may also be e-mailed to info@brickmag.com
Subscribe on-line! WWW.BRICKMAG.COM

BRICK is published twice yearly and is printed and bound
in Canada by Transcontinental Printing

Distributed in the United States by Publishers Group West

In This Issue

LEFT-HAND MAKES AND UGLY

Cover photograph of Carole Corbeil on Ontario Street, 1977 by Frank Richards, courtesy of Layne Coleman

Cover designed by Rick/Simon.

Brick logos created by David Bolduc

Please

send me
the brown coat
the one I used
to wear on
my night journeys.

W. G. Sebald

The Verbs of Boro

MARK ABLEY

anzray: to keep apart from an enemy or wicked company
mokhrob: to express anger by a sidelong glance
zum: to wear or put on clothing for the upper part of the body

I was feeling discouraged. I had spent the day ploughing through academic books about language, and not being a professional linguist, my head hurt. It appeared more and more unlikely that I would ever remember the phonetic symbol for a "lengthened, front unrounded, half-open, lax voiced vocoid" or a "voiceless, laminal post-alveolar stop with slight aspiration and a high off-glide"—because even after a fair amount of study, I couldn't recall what a lax voiced vocoid was. Linguists, like the members of most professions, have a code that excludes the uninitiated. It had begun to seem to me that the more you love language, the harder this code is to learn.

Returning to the crowded stacks of the university library, I began, almost at random, to pull books off the shelves. I didn't know exactly what I wanted—instinctively, perhaps, I was searching for some proof of humanity among those dust-dry grammars and theoretical speculations. I was looking, I suppose, for a book that would lift a language off the page. Eventually I found myself glancing through a volume published at Gauhati University, in the Indian state of Assam, in 1977: *A Descriptive Analysis of the Boro Language*. Which language was that again? I didn't know and at first I hardly cared. What caught my attention was that Pramod Chandra Bhattacharya had dedicated the book to the memory of his son Amiya Kumar, dead at the age of twelve, a boy "who is no more in this world." Dr. Bhattacharya had researched and written the volume, he said, "against a number of personal and national calamities which occurred during 1952-64"—some years before the calamity of his son's death. Humble to a fault, he offered his apologies "for my poor expressions not only in Boro, but in English."

I took the book back to my table and sat down with it.

> *egthu*: to create a pinching sensation in the armpit
> *khale*: to feel partly bitter
> *khonsay*: to pick an object up with care as it is rare or scarce

Boro, I learned, is a language of northeastern India that spills over into neighbouring countries: Nepal, Bhutan, Bangladesh. Most of its speakers live on the north bank of the Brahmaputra River. The language has other names too: Bodo, Kachari, and Mech, for a start. Whatever name you call it by, it's one of well over two hundred languages in the fertile subfamily of Tibeto-Burman. Most of these languages, being indigenous to a small area, have never had great numbers on their side—Boro is one of a handful that are used by several hundred thousand people, perhaps as many as a million. But most of its speakers are now fluent in Bengali or in Dr. Bhattacharya's mother tongue, Assamese. For any small language whose speakers lack political power and economic clout, bilingualism can be a prelude to permanent silence. The odds against Boro becoming influential are long, for it's not an official language of any nation, state, or province; bigger languages are intruding on its territory; many of its speakers suffer from extreme poverty; and most of its linguistic relatives are even smaller and more obscure.

Yet Boro has its partisans. The desire to sustain it stands at the root of a current political movement that strives to create a new Indian state of Bodo-land—or, in its most extreme form, a sovereign, fully independent nation. "Despite being the sons of the soil," one Boro leader protested in the Indian Parliament, "we people have been neglected, discriminated, oppressed, suppressed and misruled ever since Independence." A few days after my chance discovery in the library, I surfed the Internet and came across an interview with U. G. Brahma, the president of the All Bodo Students Union, who complained that "under the pressure of aggressive Sanskritization, several Bodo subgroups have forsaken the Bodo language and culture. This poses serious threat to the survival of our Bodo culture as a separate entity." It was a story familiar to me from places as far afield as Wales, Quebec, the Basque country, and Tibet: separatist movements draw their most potent energy from fears about language loss and cultural erasure. Advocates of Boro who found the students and the politicians too mild-mannered had even created a guerrilla army: the Bodo Liberation Tigers.

Unlike many endangered languages, Boro does exist in written form. Indeed it exists in two written forms: the Roman alphabet of the West and the Devanagri script of India. But the feuds between their partisans seemed to eat up far more time and anger than their common struggle against outside enemies. This too is a familiar story.

> *gobram*: to shout in one's sleep
> *khanthi*: to be wounded without bleeding
> *ur*: to dig soil (as the swine do), to move curry (while cooking)

Looking at these verbs, rolling them around in my mouth, I was reminded of the first time it ever dawned on me that languages could not be translated on an exact, word-for-word basis. As a boy, I took private French lessons from a chain-smoking spinster cousin of Albert Schweitzer's who had somehow fetched up in a basement apartment of Lethbridge, Alberta, and one day I tried to say "I am hungry." French, of course, demands not an adjective but an abstract noun: *J'ai faim*, I have hunger. Likewise I have thirst, I have fear, I have nine years. You can't just reproduce the English parts of speech; you have to recreate the idea. You have to search, often gropingly, for the best possible equivalent. For a unilingual child like me, this was a radical, scary notion. When you venture outside the confines of a mother tongue, you have to accept, even embrace uncertainty. And yet English and French are related languages with a long overlapping history and a mountain of shared vocabulary. How much harder is the search—how much rarer is a precise equivalent—when two languages have almost nothing in common? The verbs of Boro challenge me, not with *déjà vu* but with *jamais vu*.

It's not only a language of verbs, of course. Under the discreet fluorescent lights of the library ceiling, a few nouns also stood out from Dr. Bhattacharya's crinkled, yellowing pages: *bokhali*, a woman who carries a child on her back; *gansuthi*, the first grown feather of a bird's wing; *zogno*, the sound produced by a mixing of mud and water if you thrust your hand into a crab's hole. How could anyone resist a language whose expression for "slightly humpbacked" is *gobdobdob*? Boro has a whole range of terms for calling out to animals: ducks, pigeons, poultry, cats, grown-up dogs, puppies, pigs, cows, and buffalo all demand a word of their own. And in contrast to English, which asks its speakers to say "Ah!" and "Oh!" and "Hey!" in a variety of moods, Boro is blessed with twenty "interjectional exclamative particles" to express everything from insult to affection, repentance to irritation, terror to sympathy.

Unless I have severely misread Dr. Bhattacharya, though, the glory of the language lies elsewhere.

onguboy: to love from the heart
onsay: to pretend to love
onsra: to love for the last time

Verbs like these go beyond all borders: the ideas or sentiments they express transcend the culture that articulates them. I can't imagine I will ever need to express the noise that mud and water would make if I inserted my hand into a crab's hole; as far as I'm concerned, *zogno* is a word that can happily stay in Boro. While I love the surprising verb *dasa*—it means "not to place a fishing instrument"—I accept, with some reluctance, that my own language might have little use for it. But *onsay* and *onsra* are a different story. Having met those words in Dr. Bhattacharya's book, how can I do without them? I covet them, just as I covet the verbs for expressing anger by a sidelong glance or for feeling partly bitter. They are more than just fresh sounds on the tongue; they are fresh thoughts in the mind. A speaker of Boro, intimate with such words from early childhood, has quick and easy access to perceptions I am denied.

Poring for the second time over Dr. Bhattacharya's painstaking text, I recalled a passage by the Canadian lawyer Rupert Ross, whose book *Returning to the Teachings* explores some of the vexed encounters between Cree and Ojibwa people in northwestern Ontario and the forces of the Canadian justice system. Those encounters are made harder, Ross suggests, by the distinct world views that underlie the speakers' languages: "My Aboriginal friends talk a great deal about what it's like to have to use English all day, and they generally describe it as a strain. If we truly recognized that we occupy a universe of constantly transforming things, people and relationships, then we would have no choice but to discard our heavy reliance on nouns to capture and describe it." In Boro, like Cree and Ojibwa, the world appears to be constantly transforming.

Said in a different tone, Dr. Bhattacharya reports, *onsra* has a different meaning: "to arouse the female oracle for the last time."

> **gagrom:** to search for a thing below water by trampling
> **goblo:** to be fat (as a child or infant)
> **gobray:** to fall in a well unknowingly

It's possible, I admit, that a few of these words have simple English equivalents that Dr. Bhattacharya failed to find. I'm somewhat dubious about his explanation of *kholab*: "to feel tedious for an odd smell." And while I accept his faith that a

Boro proverb effectively means "An honest person is troubled," I'm still puzzling over his translation of it: "The cat clears its bowels on mild soil." Other sayings are no less earthy. Where English offers a pepperless sentence like "A great man behaves honourably," Boro conjures up a metaphor: "A big man farts straight behind."

Still, you might retort—especially if you happen to be an admirer of Noam Chomsky—the two phrases mean the same thing. In his book *Aspects of the Theory of Syntax*, Chomsky wrote: "It is possible to convey any conceptual content in any language." An extraterrestrial, he once suggested, would see all human beings as speaking a single language. Those of us rooted on Earth may be forgiven for choosing a variant perspective. As the critic George Steiner has noted, Chomsky's ideas "could account, with beautiful economy and depth, for a world in which men would all be speaking one language, diversified at most by a moderate range of dialects." In fact, however, the luxuriant profusion of tongues on the planet defies any simple notion of evolutionary benefit to our species. The incredible diversity of human languages is surely just as remarkable as the hidden similarities of their grammar. Chomsky claimed that "exciting results on universal grammar" arose from his book *Sound Patterns of English*—even though many of his examples, far from being universal, applied only to the version of the language spoken in North America.

Besides, there's more to any language that just its conceptual content. "Languages," writes Kenneth Hale, a colleague of Chomsky's at the Massachusetts Institute of Technology, "embody the intellectual wealth of the people that speak them. Losing any one of them is like dropping a bomb on the Louvre."

> **asusu**: to feel unknown and uneasy in a new place
> **gabkhron**: to be afraid of witnessing an adventure
> **serrom**: to examine by slight pressing

A quarter-century after Dr. Bhattacharya's descriptive analysis was published, linguists are again at work on the Boro language. This time their motives are zealous. "As in most animistic cultures, the Mech live in fear of the spirits of nature. Only through appeasement can they have peace or success in life, but no one is sure when or if the spirits are appeased. The Mech need liberation from such oppressive beliefs." The quotation comes from one of the "Unreached Peoples Prayer Profiles" on an American Website. After a quick sketch of traditional Boro culture, the Website requests its readers to pray: "Ask God to grant wisdom and favor to the missions agencies that are targeting the Mech." (The verb "targeting" merits some thought.) "Ask God to anoint the Gospel as it goes forth via radio in their area. . . . Ask God to speed the completion of the *Jesus* film and other Christian materials into the Bodo language."

My first instincts are to urge the Boro to use the missionaries' *asusu* and to *anzray* them, keeping *onsay* in reserve for emergencies; otherwise the Boro may soon pass beyond *khale* to a destructive *khanthi*. Yet it's not that simple. The missionaries change the culture, but the culture is changing anyway. Even rural Assam is subject to the forces of globalization, and the tribal peoples of northeastern India now face a host of pressures—environmental and economic ones among them. As well as calling for prayer to save the souls of the Boro, the missionary website warns that "A large percentage of Mech have encumbered unmanageable debt." By continuing to speak their language, they won't get rid of their debts or save their forests. But they might avoid the corrosive despair that comes when a culture implodes and disintegrates. Pride in their own tongue could give the Boro a better chance of sheer bloody survival. Who knows—the anointed Gospel and other Christian materials might even play a role in a drama of language preservation.

Otherwise, chaos beckons. "A hare dies due to its shit"—Boro sayings are not for the squeamish—"a deer dies due to its footstep; a man dies due to his mouth."

> **bunhan bunahan**: to be about to speak, and about not to speak
> **khar**: to smell like urine or raw fish
> **khen**: to hit one's heart

Stendhal's *Life of Henry Brulard*

LYDIA DAVIS

The other day I was listening to a program about astronomy on the radio, and in the space of about half-an-hour I learned at least five or six startling things, among them: that most meteors are no larger than a raisin; that a meteor the size of a grape would light up the entire sky as it descended; that if we could see him, a person poised on the edge of a black hole would appear, from the vantage point of the Earth, to hover there indefinitely, frozen in time, whereas from the vantage point of the black hole itself he would be swallowed up instantly. Some of this was hard for me to understand, and while I was still agog with it, along came the next and most disturbing comment, one concerning the nature of time: there is, they said, a good deal of evidence suggesting that at the deepest level of reality, time as we are accustomed to imagine it does not actually exist, that we live in an eternal present.

If I can comprehend it at all, this idea is not a very comfortable one. I would prefer to think of objective time as an unbroken stream of equal intervals stretching infinitely far back and far forward; then I may peaceably watch subjective time as it defies measurement by behaving in its usual capricious, elastic, elusive manner, shrinking and expanding unexpectedly or collapsing in on itself. And this was my habit of thought before I heard the radio program and while I was engrossed in reading Stendhal's *Life of Henry Brulard*. For time is very much one of the subjects of this *Life*, which remarkably transfigures or transcends it, as Stendhal looks back at his past and speaks forward in time to his readers of the future, but also, by his manner of writing, as he brings those readers into what now seems to me, after the radio program, to be an eternal present.

Stendhal wrote this strangely fragmented, digressive, and yet beautifully structured pseudonymous memoir in four quick months over the winter of 1835–1836. He had written *The Red and the Black* five years earlier, in 1830; and he was to write *The Charterhouse of Parma* (another quick book, occupying the seven weeks from early November to late December) less than two years later, in 1838. At the age of fifty-three, he is looking back at the first seventeen years of his life, at the events of what we would call—and what he would recognize as—his "formative" years, and subjecting them to a close examination and analysis "so as to work out what sort of man I have been."

Yet he is also looking ahead, contemplating and occasionally addressing the readers who will pick up his book in 1880, readers who, he thinks, may be more sympathetic to him than his contemporaries—though just as often he frets that they will be intolerably bored by the minutiae of his life. "I have no doubt had great pleasure from writing this past hour, and from trying to describe my feelings of the time *exactly as they were*," he says, "but who on earth will be brave enough to go deeply into it, to read this excessive heap of Is and mes?"

He occasionally, even, looks beyond the readers of 1880 to those of 1900, 1935, and, surprisingly, our own 2000. He is not sure, he says, if the reader of the future will still be familiar with *Les Liaisons dangereuses* by Choderlos de Laclos—yes, we still know it, we would like to answer him. He believes the reader of 1900 and one hundred years later will certainly have a more enlightened understanding of Racine. Well, there we would probably disappoint him.

Whenever we read a book, of course, time, in a sense, collapses: we feel we are reading in the same moment the writer is writing, or that we cause him to speak, and as he speaks we hear him—there is no interval; and the converse, that we have only to stop reading for a moment, and he stops speaking. What immediate authority the handwritten message of a dead parent still has! And it is true that a reader is the necessary completion of the act of writing. Yet Stendhal's *Life*, more than most, jumps beyond the bounds of its time and tradition, speaks across nearly two centuries in an intensely personal voice.

How does it achieve such immediacy? And why is this minutely detailed tabulation by this irascible grumbler so appealing?

Certainly it shares some of the qualities of other eccentric autobiographical works that continue to strike us as fresh and new despite the passage of time (if time does indeed pass): Kafka's *Letter to His Father*, Cyril Connolly's *The Unquiet Grave*, J. R. Ackerley's *Hindoo Holiday*, Gertrude Stein's *Autobiography of Alice B. Toklas*, *Roland Barthes by Roland Barthes*, Rousseau's *Confessions*, Theresa Hak Kyung Cha's *Dictée*, Michel Leiris's *Rules of the Game*. For one thing, the style of *The Life of Henry Brulard* is plain and straightforward, conversational and direct. For another, it is full of keenly observed and striking detail—a room so cold the ink freezes on the tip of the pen, a dying man carried home on a ladder, clothes "smelling of the makers."

It is written with passion. Stendhal, like the narrator of a Thomas Bernhard novel, is terribly attached to his every feeling. He is just as furious today (at the time of his writing and our reading) as he was at age fourteen, when his greatest love was mathematics ("I fancy I said to myself: *true or false, mathematics will get me out of Grenoble*, out of this mire that turns my stomach'") and he was endlessly frustrated by the complacency and hypocrisy of his teachers: what a shock, he says, "when I realized that no one could explain to me how it is that a minus times a minus equals a plus $(- \times - = +)$!" Further rage when no one will resolve another puzzle: is it or is it not true that parallel lines, when produced to infinity, will eventually meet?

Clear-eyed about his good points and bad, Stendhal aims for accuracy ("I am witty no more than once a week and then only for five minutes," he tells us), and what a complex and interesting person emerges from this self-examination. Stubborn, opinionated, cantankerous, yet brilliant, minutely observant, and appealingly fallible. Not an easy friend; someone in whose company one would be always on edge—he would be sure to pounce on any sign of fatuousness or mental sloth. Intellectually ambitious, and not merely concerning literature and politics: he still thinks he ought to study worms and beetles—"which nause-ate me"—as he had intended to do while he was a soldier fighting under Napoleon.

He has much to say about memory because he is relying entirely on that unreliable faculty in his re-creation of his early years. There is a great deal, he tells us, that he had forgotten until the present moment of writing: things come back to him that he has not thought of for decades. He often says that a certain memory is obscured because of the great emotion he experienced at the time: the emotion wiped out the memory. He points out, further, that if he remembers this much of an event, he has also forgotten a great deal more, but that if he were to begin supplementing the truth with his imagination, he would be writing a novel and not a memoir. "I protest once again that I don't claim to be describing things in themselves, but only their effect on me."

Yet *The Life of Henry Brulard* has several even more unusual features. For one thing, there are the *aide-mémoire* sketches, nearly two hundred of them, thin, spidery diagrams with scribbled explanations showing where young Stendhal was positioned in relation to others, in a room or on a mountainside, in a street or a square ("I clouted him with all my might at O"), and these sketches, minimal, crabbed, and repetitious as they are, oddly enough make his memories more real to us too.

For another, there is his abiding and multi-layered pretense at self-concealment. He not only refers to himself at points as a certain overly loquacious "Dominique," but more significantly titles the book (on the title-pages of several sections of the manuscript) as *Life of Henry Brulard written by himself* and then describes it, for the benefit of "Messrs of the police," not as an autobiography but as a novel in imitation of the very bland and innocent *Vicar of Wakefield*. Now, all the layers of the self-concealment are quite transparent: he is not Henry Brulard, he is not writing a novel, and this book does not in any obvious way resemble Goldsmith's tale. It seems unlikely that he is making a serious effort to protect himself, or even that this is merely a sustained joke. It seems more likely that the man we obligingly refer to as Stendhal, but who was of course actually Henri Beyle, and who made a habit of adopting a variety of pseudonyms in his published writings, must have been more comfortable erecting a screen of fiction behind which he could give himself permission to write with utter sincerity. There is in fact a wonderful moment well into the book where the real and the fictional names are forcibly melded in an act of sheer impudence, when Stendhal refers to "the five letters: B,R,U,L,A,R,D, that form my name."

And then, the book appears to be unfinished. Certainly it is unusually rough. Passages of expansive, fully developed narrative will be followed by a succession of terse one-sentence paragraphs, fleeting afterthoughts, qualifications, or digressions inspired by his narration—and perhaps such brief paragraphs are a perfect representation of the disconnected way in which our thoughts sometimes move. Stendhal has left blank spaces in the text where he has forgotten a name or can't think of the right adjective. He has abbreviated words freely, motivated sometimes by haste and sometimes by (he says) a fear of censorship. He includes occasional cryptic private references and secret codes. He inserts reminders to himself throughout the text, usually in the margins, or corrects errors as he goes along (below a diagram: "Entrance steps or rather no entrance steps"). He repeats himself, twice asserting, for instance, that the only passions that have remained with him throughout his life (besides the desire to write and to live in Paris) are his love of Saint-Simon and of spinach. Other marginal notes describe his present state as he writes: "18 December 1835. At 4.50, not enough daylight. I stop. . . . From 2 to half-past 4, twenty-four pages. I am so absorbed by the memories unveiling themselves to my gaze I can scarcely form my letters."

And so it is a curiosity, an anomaly: the book appears rough, unfinished, and yet there are suggestions throughout that this may be just what its author intended. I would like to know—because if Stendhal meant to leave it as it is, he has in effect written a surprisingly modern book. Did he or didn't he plan to fill in the blank spaces, write out the abbreviated words, delete the notes to himself, and in general revise and rewrite to "smooth it out"? Reading with this question in mind, I came to a clue in a marginal note: "Idea. If I don't correct this first draft, perhaps I shall manage not to tell lies out of vanity." It would seem that this thought came to him only as he was writing. Not far away another clue appeared: "I'm well aware that all of this is too

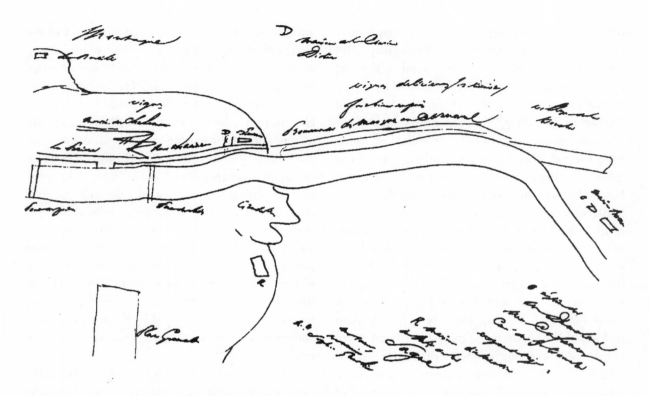

long, but I get amusement from finding these early if unhappy times reappear, and I ask M. Levavasseur to shorten it should he publish. H. Beyle." Apparently, at this point, he did not intend to go back and shorten it himself. Toward the end of the book, I came to another: "I shall perhaps have to reread and emend this passage, contrary to my intentions. . . ." (The book ends with seven drafts of "Testaments" bequeathing the manuscript to a host of possible publishers, including the bookseller Levavasseur, with instructions to publish it fifteen years after Stendhal's death with all the women's names changed and none of the men's.)

Why is the fragmented, the rough, sometimes so much more inviting than the seamless, the polished? Because we are closer to the moment of creation? ("Handwriting," he notes in a margin. "This is how I write when my thoughts are treading on my heels. . . .") Because we are intimate witnesses to the formulation of the thought? Inside the experience of the writer instead of outside? Because we are closer to the evolution by which an event of the past, long forgotten—though evidently somewhere present in the brain cells of the writer—is reawakened, reimagined, re-presented, put into words? ("My heart is pounding still as I write this thirty-six years later. I abandon my paper, I wander round my room and I come back to writing.") As though we were taking part ourselves, involved in and identifying with the action, the action being in this case the re-creation and understanding of a life?

Perhaps, too, a work that comes to us so fresh, so raw, from the writer's mind is more exciting because we see how precarious is the writer's control—the material is almost more powerful than he is. As Stendhal himself says, it was the material—his ideas, his memories—that commanded him, not some "literary ideal." And so it is a work that changes as he writes it, that is full of his own discovery as he goes along; and for his own purposes, and to our delight, he notes the elaboration of this memoir even as he writes it.

At one point in his narration Stendhal refers casually to a moment later in his life when he was in mortal danger: alone in a Silesian field, he saw coming toward him a company of Cossacks. He does not go on to tell us what happened next. I wondered, as I continued reading, whether he was merely being artful and would satisfy my curiosity before the book ended. I suspected he would not, and he did not. His intention in the book, after all, is not to tell a dramatic story. Yet a different, and greater, drama unfolds as we read, because of the constant double surprise: being alongside him as he works, rather than being handed the result of a later revision, we surprise him in the very act of writing even as he surprises himself in the act of remembering and understanding. And so we are privileged to watch what is really the very dramatic moment, enacted again and again, of the unremembered or half-remembered being fully brought to mind, the unformed being formed, the internal becoming external, the private becoming public.

Pictures at a Demonstration

MAGGIE HELWIG

The first thing you hear clearly on the video, oddly enough, is my voice.

A crowd of people in jeans and sweaters, some with ripped T-shirts and spiked hair, are milling around a large park. People are carrying cardboard signs or unfolding canvas banners. From somewhere off-camera, I am saying, in a tired and irritable way, "If you see Anita, tell her she's speaking. Mike McHenry never showed up."

"Okay," says the cameraman vaguely, his mind on his work.

The cameraman is my friend David Maltby, and the gathering is the beginning of a protest march against ARMX, a weapons trade fair being held in Ottawa, in the late spring of 1989. I was one of the protest organizers. That day, two or three thousand people marched to the exhibition grounds where the fair was to take place. The next morning, as it opened, about 150 of us were arrested while blocking the entrance gates. David filmed it all—the march, the rally, the meetings that night, and the blockade at one of the gates the next day.

Over the years David and I talked, on and off, about editing his footage into a proper documentary, making it tighter and smoother, adding interviews, political context. He gave me the tapes, which I carried with me to many different houses, but we never did get around to sitting down and editing them.

In May 2001, David died, suddenly, horribly, of bacterial meningitis. I do not have the knowledge or talent to edit his footage myself, and I'm not sure that I would want anyone else to do it. What follows, then, are some notes towards a film that will never be made.

There were huge changes in the air that spring, and on some level, all of us knew it. *Glasnost* and *perestroika* had suddenly become familiar words, the stuff of editorial cartoons. On the bus to Ottawa, one of the organizers read out stories of the Tiananmen Square protests from the newspaper. We didn't know, of course, that Tiananmen Square would end in a terrible night of tanks and blood, but I think that we were not so very surprised. It was how one expected these things to end.

We also didn't know that, just months later, young people would come surging over the Berlin Wall, and the Cold War—the international condition that had lasted longer than many of us had lived—would end in what seemed like a single astonishing moment. Despite the sense of changes coming, this was something we never expected. Never, I think, believed possible.

In 1989, international politics were still Cold War politics. The cornerstone was Mutual Assured Destruction, the ability of both the U.S.A. and the U.S.S.R. to blow the world up several times over. At least twenty companies involved in the manufacture of nuclear weapons would exhibit at ARMX.

Most wars were still the proxy wars of the superpowers. Chile had made its first tentative move toward democracy, but Pinochet had not yet stepped down. Representatives of the Pinochet regime had attended the previous ARMX, in 1987, and most likely purchased weaponry. Brutal wars against the civilian population were raging in El Salvador and Guatemala and East Timor—and the governments involved were all buyers of Canadian military equipment or components. In 1989 in El Salvador, 47,000

civilians were murdered; in Guatemala, 100,000. The apartheid regime was still in power in South Africa, Nelson Mandela still in prison. The Contra force was still wreaking terror in Nicaragua with sophisticated weapons obtained from the United States. NATO had plans to build a massive training base on unceded Native territory in Labrador.

It was with this background that we marched.

In the park, crowds assemble behind banners— mostly hand-painted, a few beautifully tie-dyed— and begin to march from the park. As David walks up and down the edges of the march, we can see that it is a fairly diverse group. Not everyone is young by any means, and some are quite well dressed. There are parents with small children. There are Quakers and Catholics. There are the Trinity-Spadina NDP and the Young Liberals for Peace. There is a middle-aged couple who have, for some reason, wrapped themselves in a quilt; there are teenagers with painted faces. Buses and cars of demonstrators have come from Hamilton, Kitchener, Kingston, Peterborough, Montreal.

A group of Salvadoran women march near the front, at first—later, they are displaced by the Black Bloc. But it was a more innocent time, I guess; the Black Bloc members of 1989 do not throw Molotov cocktails. All they really do to distinguish themselves is to dress in black, wear scarves over their faces, and push their way in front of the Salvadoran women. David walks with the Black Bloc for a while; they have a flautist and some drummers, and are certainly the most musical section of the march.

As the march travels down Bank Street, David stops and films two men sitting in a greasy spoon, looking out the window. The men do not move at all during the several minutes that he films them; one of them appears tired and bored, the other stares at the street with an expression of bewildered disgust as the demonstrators file past him. It is a remarkably stable expression; his face hardly twitches, no matter who is passing him, and David films him for some while. It's hard to tell if he notices that he is being filmed, but I think he must

have known, and part of his mysterious immobility must have been simply embarrassment.

The march goes on for a long time; it was a lengthy march, through the centre of Ottawa and out to Lansdowne Park, and it was even more tedious in real life than it seems on the video. Still, the marchers are mostly in good spirits. There is a brief flurry of mass hysteria as we pass under a highway bridge, and everyone, carried away by the echo, begins to scream and clap and pound on the concrete walls—David spins the camera in circles, hoping to capture the giddiness that has overtaken us. As I recall, we acted like this because we thought we were nearly at the stadium, and when we came out from under the bridge and found that we were only just past the halfway point, we became rather discouraged and subdued.

Every now and then the action is interrupted, as David points the camera to the sky. At these times, you can hear what sounds like heavy breathing on the tape. In fact these are the moments when David, who was a severe and chronic asthmatic, is using his inhaler. In a proper documentary, of course, these moments would have to be edited out. But to me they are precious, a reminder of my sometimes fragile friend.

David was tall and very thin and very pale, with blond hair falling down past his shoulders, a long thin nose, light blue eyes, a quick soft smile. I met him when we were both working at the *Varsity*, the University of Toronto student paper, though neither of us were actually students at that time; we were a few years older than the others, the real students, but I guess we were taking a longer time to grow up. Anyway, we covered the alternative music beat together. Later, we managed to involve ourselves in Tent City, a Student Christian Movement protest against the G-7 summit in Toronto, where we met Vannina, a major character later in the ARMX video, and Brian, another ARMX organizer, though he does not show up in the video as much.

Today Vannina has two children, and is working on a Ph.D. I have one child and I am writing books. Brian's son had already started school at the time of ARMX; Brian is now a priest of the Old Catholic Church and works in social housing. All of us still consider ourselves political activists, though I suppose we are tired and somewhat cynical activists now.

"It's so strange," says Vannina, when I play the video for her. "We sound like such young naive people. Which I guess is what we were." Yet Vannina had grown up in Uruguay, and among her early memories is one day when her parents went out to a demonstration, and she heard gunfire in the streets and didn't know if they would come home. A small child, afraid, she tried to calm herself by repeating, "It's only fireworks. It's only fireworks."

It was Brian who phoned, that spring, to tell me that David was in the hospital; he had heard it second-hand, from someone who knew David's landlady. Brian didn't know clearly what was wrong, but he had been told that David was in a coma.

I paced up and down the living room for half an hour, and decided that I had to go to the hospital. At the reception desk, they told me that he was in intensive care, but that it might be possible to visit.

I went up one floor to the intensive care unit. From the elevator to the ICU, I walked through a long low corridor, almost like the passageway from an airport to a plane. There was the same sense of separation from the world, entering another kind of reality. At the end of the corridor, the ICU waiting room. I remember that there were blue chairs. Some people had brought pillows. There was no one there I recognized.

I wandered around the room, uncertain what to do. Signs gave brief instructions about visiting hours, and there were binders by the telephone with basic information about certain illnesses and accidents. Reference material for phone calls. I wonder now how they chose which conditions to include and which to leave out. I didn't know what had happened to David, so there was nothing for me to look up.

There was a telephone on the wall, with instructions to dial 3 if you wanted to visit someone in the ICU. I dialed 3 and was told I could go in.

In the ICU hallway, David's brother-in-law came out to meet me. "It's not looking good," he said. "It's not looking good at all."

The front of the march reaches Lansdowne Park. The police have used metal barricades to fence off an area in the parking lot for the rally, but they didn't expect a fraction of the number of people who have come, and the area is far too small. It is at this point that the members of the Black Bloc take their one definite action. Grabbing the metal barricades, they run with them, and push them to the outer edges of the parking lot. The barricades will stand there for the remainder of the rally.

There are scattered cheers from the other marchers. It strikes me, watching the video now, that turning a small fenced-off space into a somewhat larger fenced-off space is a specifically Canadian kind of anarchist victory.

Most of the rally is not on the video; only a few minutes here and there from some of the speakers. If the march was long, the rally seemed interminable, and in fact I remember almost nothing about it. Quite possibly I had wandered away with

friends. I was never much of a person for listening to speeches.

The ubiquitous sellers of *Socialist Worker* wander up and down the edges of the crowd while Audrey McLaughlin brings greetings from the Yukon. Meanwhile, reporters sit at the edge of the stage going over their notes, Ottawa city workers put the finishing touches on a new razor-wire barrier at the top of the fence, and activists from different groups stand around the barricades and criticize each other. (This last is not something you can hear on the tape, but I've been part of the movement long enough that I don't need to hear it to know it was happening.)

The last speaker urges everyone to come to a meeting that night to plan for the blockade tomorrow. It will, she says, be held at St. Peter's Seminary. The video resumes in the middle of this meeting. A few hundred people are sitting or lying on the floor of a nondescript gymnasium, listening to three of the organizers who are standing at the front of the room. No one looks happy.

The part of the meeting that is saved on video is a long discussion about bail conditions, about who is willing to sign, as a condition of their release, a promise not to return to the ARMX site, and who would prefer to stay in jail. The discussions are mostly subdued and muttered. The one moment of animation comes when someone from Kitchener raises his hand and asks for an agreement on when the meeting will end, and everyone else breaks into spontaneous applause.

Most people are sitting with their affinity groups —small groups who will be responsible for blockading different gates into the site. Most of the affinity

groups have been put together by location, everyone from Hamilton for instance. There is also a Christian affinity group, and for this action I am part of a women-only affinity group. This is not because of any separatist leanings; it is mostly because some of us didn't want to be anywhere near a few of the male organizers, and this seemed like the most tactful way to avoid them. We have, however, not only agreed to have David videotape the action at our gate, we have made him nearly an official member of the group.

After the meeting—finally, mercifully—winds down and concludes, the various affinity groups meet together, mostly clustered in circles on the lawn of the building. In the women's affinity group, we decide there are enough people planning to be arrested that we can divide into two groups—when the first group has been taken away from the gate, the second group will move in, so we will be able to blockade the site for a bit longer. David turns the camera off.

And then the film resumes, and it is morning. The feeling of the morning meeting is quite different. No one had slept terribly well—some people had gone to bars in Hull and stayed there until three in the morning, the rest of us were just lying on piles of coats on the floor of the gym. But everyone is alert, tense. We are dealing with things that are concrete and immediate now. Someone has been to the site by bicycle, and is briefing us on which gates are being used.

It seems that Lansdowne Park has closed all but two of the entrance gates. The affinity groups assigned to the closed gates have been asked to lock them down with kryptonite locks, and then wait to be reassigned to a gate that is open. The two gates currently being used are Gate Two, where the rally was held yesterday, and Gate Nine, where the women's group has been assigned.

I am sitting cross-legged near the front of our group, in a navy blue jacket and a beige cap. When I watch the video now, my face seems to me absurdly soft and young. I have a sign around my neck that says "Anna Mae Aquash: Murdered by FBI." One of the many theatrical props the women's group has brought is these signs, in memory of women killed in wars around the world.

Today, as a matter of fact, we know that Anna Mae Aquash was killed by the American Indian Movement—by her own people. I could not have known that at the time, I have to remind myself. No one knew then, except the people who had been there. I suppose that no matter who killed Anna Mae, she was in some way a casualty of militarized masculinity, so there is a way in which the sign still makes sense; but I do believe in accuracy, and I would rather, now, that I was not wearing it. There are a lot of ways we would all like to revise our lives, if we could. Maybe it is a good thing that the sign was captured on video.

This is probably where I would start the video, if I was editing it. It is a bright morning in May as we march out into the street. Grass and trees seem sharply, vividly green. It is a much smaller march than the day before, and overall much younger. Though a few people who will be arrested are in their sixties or seventies, most of us are under thirty. I am twenty-seven years old, David is twenty-six, Vannina twenty-three.

We file over a bridge, through a park, passing under a canopy of leaves. Vannina and I walk together, our heads bent in conversation. Others file past the camera—Karen, Joanne, Frank, many whose names I can't remember now. David holds the camera behind a banner, the sunlight shining through the white cloth, catching a red drop of painted blood, shimmering in the early morning as it is carried across the grass.

David positions himself beside a reporter, who is phoning in what sounds like a live story for radio. He films the leaves of the trees while he records the man talking. "The demonstrators who marched down Bank Street yesterday vowed to return this morning, and indeed they are. The first of them are now at about Fifth Avenue and they should be approaching the gates of Lansdowne Park any moment now."

Gate Nine is the first gate we reach. It faces a residential street: small houses, painted white or red. Most of the groups keep walking, but our affinity group, and David's camera, will stop here.

David and I ended up doing a lot of things together at the *Varsity*, because we had tastes that were—at least by the standards of the University of Toronto—weird and avant-garde, and because we liked to stage photographs (Eugene Chadbourne attacking me with a plastic chainsaw; me dressed up as a motorcycle babe in spandex) and draw funny faces on negatives. We covered a lot of things together, not just music; we went together to interview Al Purdy, John Waters, Susan Sontag. After the interview with Al Purdy, David stole an ashtray and a spoon and a glass from the Silver Dollar, because Purdy had touched them I guess, so they had become relics of a sort.

We had a project, for a while, of getting famous people to autograph books they hadn't written. We never got very far with it, but I do remember the two of us hanging around backstage at Ildiko's, trying to convince a fairly prominent punk musician to sign a science fiction paperback.

It was an important friendship for me. When I met David, I was just recovering from anorexia. I was a small and frightened person, and not very easy to get along with, but in him I recognized, almost right away, someone it was possible to trust. I'm not even sure what it was that I feared; probably just that everyone would laugh at me. I didn't really understand, in those days, how people managed to relate to each other—they all seemed to be guided by complex and secret codes that I couldn't fathom, and I always suspected that if I tried to talk

to anyone, I would get it all wrong and seem ridiculous. But David was open, transparent; someone I could understand, someone I could feel safe with.

In the summer of 1988 we drifted onto the Tent City organizing committee. "I never really knew where you came from," says Vannina now. "I mean, we were all students, and then suddenly you and David showed up. I never figured that out. But it was good. It made it different than it would have been."

David had an odd way of moving sometimes— swaying or hovering, like he was being blown around by the wind. He alternated, in those days, between antic silliness and melancholy. He carried his cameras everywhere and laughed, at himself, at the world.

After Tent City was broken up by the police, we marched down University Avenue with the main anti-G-7 protest, three thousand people or so walking up to the barricades and the riot police, snipers on the rooftops around us, and David was almost dancing in the middle of the crowd, long hair flying, switching from a still camera to a video and back again, running backwards in front of advancing lines of police, dodging between demonstrators and barricades, elated, intense. Taking pictures.

Outside the doors of the ICU, David's brother-in-law told me about the diagnosis, described what I would see if I went inside. "Do you still want to go in?" he asked.

I looked through the doors. I thought—I have come this far. Whatever choice I make now, there will be no reversing it. I thought—I have to see him for myself. I have to know.

"Yes," I said. "I'd like to go in."

There is confusion in front of Gate Nine. It becomes clear that, although we thought we had things organized last night, every single woman who is planning to blockade believes that she is in the second wave. In a crowd of police and reporters and support demonstrators, we try to figure out what we are doing next; and meanwhile, dark cars are driving into the ARMX site.

The camera veers up to the sky again as David reaches for his inhaler; then back down to the scene at the gate. "We shall overcome . . ." someone sings weakly, her voice trailing away.

Finally, I decide that, lacking any other solution, I will be the first wave. I walk to the gateway and stand in the middle. Since it is about eight feet wide, I am not able to block it very effectively. I grab a ball of red wool from one of the support people, and begin to string it from one end of the gate to the other. Joanne helps me tie it to the metal posts. Joanne is a retired schoolteacher whose husband died of multiple cancers after being exposed to a radioactive spill at the Eldorado uranium refinery, where he worked.

When the next car comes to the gate, I jump in front of it; the security guards push me away. David is being jostled, can't get near the gate; there is just a brief glimpse of me, my arms full of wool, being bundled away to the edge of the fence.

David pans over the crowd. Vannina is by herself a few yards away, tying signs to the fence. I am standing in front of another car; the security guards push me away again. "Wool!" I call out, stepping away from the gate for a second. "Somebody toss me some more wool!" A ball of wool flies toward me, and I return to the gate.

Another car drives up, and again I stand in front of it. This time it is the Ottawa police who take hold of me. For a moment we are all motionless, the car and the police and me, and then they begin to pull on my arms. My legs twist as I try to brace myself in the dirt, but of course they are stronger than I am. Two policemen drag me away. We disappear behind a line of parked cars. "Yay Maggie," says someone. almost absent-mindedly.

"I guess," says someone else, "that we should sit down now."

It was not only the asthma that made David seem fragile; and not only that he was thin and fair and fine-featured. There was something about him, a sadness that was too often self-destructive, a kind of worry that drained away his strength. At any given time, he could list for you a dozen ways in which he was emotionally messed up, and as many things that he was trying to do to get his life in order. There were failed relationships that he couldn't get over. There was the time he had unprotected sex in a bathhouse, and the obsessive worry that followed and probably did him more damage than the sex itself. There was a spell in rehab for "substance abuse problems." Constant intentions to get organized, to work regularly. To get over being flighty and confused and chaotic.

If I had been told that he would die young, there

is a part of me that would not have been surprised. But the real irony, the thing that made that day in the ICU so strange, is that he did get his life in order. Maybe not in a way that everyone would have recognized—he still lived near the poverty line in an attic apartment and dressed in layers of tattered sweaters and jackets and scarves—and only slowly, only by tiny increments. But he did start working regularly, organizing his portfolio, getting himself the kind of equipment he needed. He did have a photo-spread in the *Globe and Mail*, the beginning of a reputation. There was something, a solidity, that he was starting to gather inside himself. He swayed less, I suppose. The last time I saw him he seemed simply happy; happy in a calm and unremarkable way, maybe for the first time since I'd known him.

At one of the memorial services after his death, I saw a photo of him that I hadn't seen before. It had been taken about a year earlier, at a demonstration that had turned violent. This picture seems to record the moment when things began to fall apart. David is standing at a metal barricade, a line of riot police behind it. Young men in black, their faces masked, are rushing the barricades, trying to tear them down. David stands in the middle of this, facing the camera. One hand holds his own camera sideways, aiming at the police. The other hand is extended, palm outwards, toward someone off-camera: a warning gesture, I think. His face is unusually stern, almost grim, and he looks—there is no other way I can think to say this—grown-up. He looks like a tall, strong man, not so thin anymore, an island of stability in a crazy place.

Not long after the photo was taken, a police-man, lashing out indiscriminately, clubbed David in the head. But he survived that, too. In one of our last conversations he told me he was trying to decide "whether to go to Quebec and get my head bashed in again." He did go to Quebec, to the FTAA meeting; like everyone else, demonstrators and reporters and bystanders, he was teargassed. He kept on taking photographs. They would be his last major piece of work.

There are ten women sitting in the gate now, clapping and chanting "Disarm ARMX!" and "Take the toys away from the boys!" They are wrapping themselves and the fence in multicoloured strands of wool. In front of them on the ground is a litter of signs, flowers, and small wooden crosses.

David is able to get quite close to the gate, almost sitting with the women as they continue their blockade. Cars have quickly backed up all the way down the street. The ARMX delegates leave their vehicles and make their way into the site on foot, men and a few women dressed in black and dark blue stepping over the women sitting in the gate and their woolen barricade.

A slight young woman with red hair is sitting at the far right-hand side, holding up a piece of cloth with the name of a Timorese resistance fighter, killed years ago. As people climb over the wool, she stretches out her cloth, moves a bit further to the right so that they will have to climb over her body instead. The police take hold of her, and she is the second person to be arrested.

The others spread out to fill the gap, chanting "ARMX kills!," but delegates keep climbing over them. As they pass Karen, she gets right up beside them and shouts, "Hey! You got blood on your hands! You got blood on your hands, man!" Karen will attract the camera's attention often throughout the day, both because she is uncommonly pretty— small, plump, dark-skinned, compact—and because she has a great deal of dramatic flair. She is dressed in a tight-fitting orange shirt; a white scarf waves from her neck. "You got blood on your hands!" she shouts at men in suits as they enter the site.

A man tries to walk past a white-haired woman sitting on the ground. She reaches out to Joanne, who is standing beside her, and grabs her arm, so that if he wants to go by he will have to force these two elderly women apart. Joanne smiles up at him, talks to him, a bit ruefully but with no intention of being moved.

"Hey Vannina! Hey Vannina!" someone is shouting, as Vannina unpacks balls of wool and throws them to the other women. Wool sails through the air, from one side of the gate to the other.

A very young security guard, surely not more than twenty, is pulling the wool from the posts. "It's on this side of the fence, it's mine now!" he shouts at someone out of sight, yanking viciously at the wool. He looks frightened, and he looks like the kind of person whom fear makes mean in petty ways.

Now the police decide to clear the gate, and women are dragged or carried away one after the other, trailing long ribbons of wool behind them. The police are irritated by the wool, which makes it much harder to separate women from each other and from the fence; they kick and tear at the strands. David follows some of the women from the gate as far as he dares go into the site. Each woman is photographed by police, and then placed on a bus.

There is a momentary break in the blockade; only one member of the women's group is left now, the white-haired woman; the police are reluctant to drag her. It is easy for people to walk in (the cars, ironically, are blocked off mostly by a ring of cameramen). But this lasts only for a few seconds. Almost before the gap is noticeable, the Kitchener group rush forward and sit down. Vannina throws balls of wool toward them, and they too begin to weave themselves into place.

The thing that I can't remember is how long the hallway was, from the doors into the ICU to David's room. Somehow it seems as if I walked a long way when I was going in; but when I was leaving, the doors were only a few feet from the room. I really don't know which memory is accurate. I can't seem to reconcile them.

Here are a few other memories, at random: coming home and finding David's voice on my answering machine, singing, "Hey, I'm a sensitive guy / I can't do much, but I sure know how to cry"; the two of us sitting on the roof of a gallery on King Street, looking down at the city; the little happy faces with spiky hair he drew in one of my books. We didn't see each other as often as we had, the last few years—I had a child, I didn't get out much, I lost touch with most people. But he was there, he was at the other end of the phone, part of my life.

Some things you remember clearly, and others you just can't get straight. I would have almost no memories of ARMX at all, if it weren't for the video.

One by one, the members of the Kitchener group are dragged away, including a man in a dark suit with a briefcase. The Hamilton group takes their place, and they too are dragged off. After the Hamilton people are gone, the security guards push the gate closed, and in one of those absurdly symbolic moments, they trap a brown plastic baby doll under the wires. The crowd goes momentarily wild, pointing at the doll, pushing themselves up against the fence and screaming, "That's exactly what this is all about! Murderers!" Cameramen race to the fence to get a picture of the doll. "Shut it down, shut it down!" yells the crowd.

But almost as soon as the gate is closed, the guards get word that they must open it again, that none of the other gates are operational. So once again they pull the doors open, and right away a large man in a pink T-shirt lies down across the entrance. He is dragged away, and four more people take his place.

Things move quickly now. Groups of two, three, or four people, or sometimes single individuals, will move into the gateway, often lying down in front of cars. The police will drag them away almost immediately, and more people will come forward.

Groups are arriving now from other gates, closed gates. Everything is happening here and at Gate Two, the only working entrances. Some of the people who live across the street have also come out to see what's happening. One neighbourhood resident, a middle-aged man in a grey suit and an eccentric-looking fedora, is wandering around and bumping into the police in an obviously deliberate way.

Three men with colourful ponchos and headbands, who look as if they have arrived directly from Woodstock, lie down at the gate. As one of them is dragged away, he pulls himself up and shouts, "Stop the bloodshed in the Third World countries!" It is not his fault that this sounds rehearsed, and more than a bit comical. One of the security guards wears sinister dark glasses, talks into his collar, and smirks frequently; he is living in a movie too, no doubt, just a different one.

The guards are checking passes now as people clamber or push their way inside. David is warned several times to step back off the property. Invariably, like the other cameramen, he apologizes, steps back, then walks right onto the property again. One photographer, from Canadian Press I think, gets involved in a scuffle with the security guard in dark glasses. David's camera veers around chaotically sometimes as he is shoved back behind police lines.

A man in a wheelchair, a small blonde girl covering her mouth with her hands, a woman in a black T-shirt, a red-haired man in a bright blue vinyl windbreaker—all are carried away, one by one.

The police cannot tolerate the man in the fedora anymore, and drag him off to the bus. Unlike the demonstrators, he struggles and argues, but they push him along, photograph him, and force him on board.

The blockade becomes more sporadic now. Cars are entering the gate, the support people held back by lines of police. Every few minutes, a person or two will make an impulsive decision, dash out in front of the cars, and be dragged away to the bus. Karen stands in the road, moving her arms in elegant, dance-like gestures, directing the cars away from the gate. "You're going the wrong way. You're going the wrong way, man."

There is much that is silly about us. I would never try to deny that. And I won't spend a lot of time here in self-justification; that's not what this is about.

But I will tell one story. In 1988, the Iraqi military rained mustard gas, nerve gas, cyanide, and phosphorus on villages of Kurdish civilians. They used, for this purpose, military training aircraft converted to attack craft. An Amnesty International report on the incident speaks of "dozens of people, blistered and burned, stumbling silently from a stricken village.... [People arriving in the village] found a small boy and girl clinging to each other. . . . They had come under attack from an Iraqi helicopter and become separated from their parents. The parents had died but the children did not know this. They kept saying that when it grew light they would go and look for them. They thought it was night. They did not real-

ize that they were blind." The planes used engines from Pratt & Whitney, a Canadian company. A prominent exhibitor, of course, at ARMX.

One driver does not slow down when he sees people on the ground, is about to hit them when the police manage to pull him to a halt. "You'll have to wait for us to clear them away, sir," says a police officer patiently. "You can't just run over them."

"Why not? Why not?" fumes the driver. "I mean, it's my car."

A pretty black-haired woman in a white dress will be the seventy-sixth, and last, person arrested at this gate. About as many are arrested at Gate Two. It all takes just over an hour. Not long after the last arrest, the guards decide that all the delegates are inside and close the gate again, only cracking it open slightly to allow a few stragglers through.

"You have a choice!" Liza shouts through the fence. "Get into therapy, work it out! Really, think about it, I think therapy would be very helpful!"

David and another cameraman find themselves filming each other. David's goofy laugh wells up behind the camera. "C'mon," says the other man, "you make funny faces when you shoot, too."

A man with a press pass coming through the gate—coming out, not in—whispers to Karen, "I've got some stuff for you," and she moves away from the main group to talk to him.

"Are you proud of what you do?" Rod quietly asks a man who is entering the site. "Really, are you proud of what you do?"

Karen returns to the group; the man with the press pass has given her a box full of catalogues, promotional materials, press releases. She stands in front of the closed gate, opens a glossy brochure and reads. David films her from below, the mid-morning sun shining around her and the tall policemen lined up behind her.

"On behalf of the Government of Canada and the Department of National Defence, I am pleased to welcome all visitors and exhibitors to ARMX 89. The Canadian Forces look to advanced technology to provide efficient and cost-effective military strength. According to ARMX 89—I mean—Accordingly, ARMX 89 provides a forum which allows state-of-the-art training devices and procedures to be viewed and discussed amongst specialists from industry, government, and military. I am encouraged by those participating in ARMX 89. This representation will promote new ideas, new technologies, and operations amongst participants. Such as Chile and South Africa."

"Does it really say that?" asks Vannina.

"Not the part about Chile and South Africa," admits Karen. "That's what's between the lines." She resumes reading. "I invite all exhibitors to visit the Canadian Forces booth and meet our military representatives, who are looking forward to reviewing your displays. I congratulate Baxter Publications and the *Canadian Defence Quarterly* on their efforts in organizing and sponsoring this exhibition. To all participants I extend my personal best wishes for every success in blowing up the world."

That is where I would end the video, I think. The unedited footage, of course, does not end there. In fact, David followed Karen, Vannina, and a few oth-

ers to the police station, where they waited outside to see when those of us who had been arrested would be released (not until late that night, as it turned out; and we were released from the court house, not from the police station). He filmed them for about half an hour, sitting on benches outside the station, looking through catalogues at "families" of tanks and tank guns, and having the kind of conversations that well-meaning young activists have—"They just look down on us, you know, because we're not so well dressed. But we look like most people, really. I mean, we could get all dressed up in, like, polyester or something; but then we'd just be buying into their value system, wouldn't we?" Eventually, he turned the camera off.

I walked the long, or short, distance of the hallway. The ICU rooms were tightly clustered around the central nurses' station. David's room, like the others, was divided in two sections by a glass wall. In the outer room there were charts, signs, tables, some equipment. David's sister Sue was here, and a nurse, a small Chinese woman in orange scrubs. There were some takeout sandwiches lying on a chair.

Inside I could see only a bed surrounded by machines, and David's other sister, Patty, in a gown and a mask, talking quietly and constantly.

"You can go in if you want," said Sue. I nodded, and kept standing outside. After a while Sue and her husband went to pick up some things from her office.

"If you want to go in, you have to put on a gown," said the nurse. "And a mask. And if you're going to touch him you have to wear gloves."

I stood outside. I didn't know what was appropriate. I thought maybe I should leave this to his family; I didn't want to make myself more important than I really was.

But I couldn't see him from the outer room, and I wanted to see him. I thought that it was possible that he would hear my voice. I put on the green gown; then I had trouble with the mask, got it on wrong the first time, and I had to go out of the room and adjust it and go back in. I looked at the box of gloves and thought, no. This is what I won't do, what I will leave to the family only.

Patty was still standing over the bed. "Maggie's coming in now," she said to David.

He was lying on the bed, and the first thing that struck me was that his shoulders were broader than they used to be.

I had read about meningitis, about the rash of purple bruises that form under the skin, but I had never seen it before. Dark, sporadic, violent.

The thick plastic tube of a ventilator pushed his lips apart. There was blood on his mouth, bright red. There was a thin trail of blood running out of his ear.

I knew, then, that he was not coming back. It didn't seem right to say goodbye, at least not to use that word. But I did know that this was the last time I would speak to him.

I didn't say much. I still think about this—I wonder if I should have stayed longer, said more. I wonder if I shouldn't have come at all. I guess I was only there for a minute or two.

"I love you," I said.

I came out of the room and the nurse told me to wash my hands. I did, and then I realized I hadn't taken off the gown, and I had to go back into the room to discard it. Then I sat in a chair for a while, my head in my hands. Patty was wiping the blood from David's ear with a piece of cotton wool.

I stood up and walked the short, or long, distance to the doors.

They sit on the benches, in front of a slope of grass, wrapped in sunlight. Vannina, Karen, Ruth, Mary.

We are ferociously idealistic. We believe in all good and great things. We are innocent and undamaged and immortal.

Behind the camera, David's rising laugh.

A Conversation with Walter Murch

MICHAEL ONDAATJE

*The following is from an on-going conversation I've had over the last two years with the film editor Walter Murch (*The Conversation, Apocalypse Now Redux, The English Patient*). During the process we covered subjects as diverse as directing, music, literature, film editing, and that art's relationship to writing. The interview below shows Murch's interest in the Italian poet and novelist Curzio Malaparte. The interviews will appear this fall under the title* The Conversations: Walter Murch and the Art of Editing Film*

Murch's translation of Malaparte's poem "Sleepwalking" follows the interview.*

MO: I want to talk about you and Curzio Malaparte's writing. Tell me how you got interested in him? Did you learn Italian in order to translate him?

WM: I had taken a year of Italian in college. So I had a pre-existing interest in Italian. And I speak French—I like the Romance languages.

Then, in 1986 when we were in Lyons shooting the invasion of Prague for *The Unbearable Lightness of Being*, I ran out of things to read.

I went to a French bookstore and bought a book on cosmology. The author was explaining the very early stages of the universe after the Big Bang, and he wrote, "I could try to tell you about this moment, but it's better simply to recount Malaparte's story about the frozen horses of Lake Ladoga."

The story involved the siege of Leningrad, artillery bombardments, forest fires, hundreds of cavalry horses on a frenzied escape from the flames only to end up flash-frozen as they reached the supercooled water of the lake. And to top it off, all this somehow related to the condition of the universe shortly after the Big Bang. I loved it! I had to find out who this Malaparte was.

Back in Berkeley, I went to the university library and found the three works of his that are translated into English, one of which was *Kaputt*, which contains the story of the frozen horses. Reading the rest of the book was like falling into a waking dream. I read everything I could get my hands on after that, including works that had not been translated into English.

After *The English Patient*, in the course of an interview with the magazine *Parnassus*, I compared the process of adaptation to translation, in the sense that many of the decisions you make—when you go from a book to a script and then from a script to shooting and from shooting to editing—are like translating from one language to another, from the language of words to the language of images and sounds. But there is naturally within each language a different emphasis on certain things. You have to take that difference into account when you translate from one language to another.

After the interview was over, I thought, hmm, it sounds good but maybe I'd better do some translation to make sure that what I'm saying is true. So I went back to some of the Malaparte material that was only in Italian. I was happy to discover that translation was a very congenial operation for me, particularly right after having finished a film. You're so keyed up in making the film that when it's over, suddenly, after a year of work, you feel like you've fallen off the edge of a cliff. To continue that work, in a different form, was a very pleasing way to make the transition back to the non-film way of living.

MO: But Malaparte is essentially a prose writer and you're translating his prose into poetry. What's your reason for that?

WM: It seemed to happen all by itself. It surprised me because I'm not somebody who naturally gravitates to poetry. I prefer to read prose, if given the choice. So I was surprised, but because it seemed to happen automatically I let it.

With hindsight, I'd say there are probably the rich, almost overwhelming density of Malaparte's original text; the fabulous nature of his imagery; his frequent use of repetitions; and the cross-sensory nature of his metaphors ("the air filled with water and stone," "a bitter blue light").

MO: The politics of his life seem very complicated and ambivalent. We are never too sure where he stands. He's constantly changing sides.

WM: Complicated is putting it mildly! His real name was Kurt Suckert—his father was a German who had married a girl from Milan. So he was Protestant German in an Italian Catholic world. He ran away from home at age sixteen and fought all four years of the First World War on the side of the French against the Germans. He was so disturbed by what happened during the war that he joined the Italian Fascist party in its early, idealistic phase. Later on, he was expelled for writing an expose of Mussolini's rise to power after he felt that the original ideals had been corrupted. After World War II he became a Communist, and then on his deathbed he converted to Catholicism, apparently.

His adopted name—Malaparte—could be read as the "bad part" that does not fit in with the rest of society. There's still a great deal of controversy about him in Italy. Some see him as an egotistical opportunist. I think there's something else going on, a bruised idealism that could never find a home in this imperfect world.

I think one of the reasons his writing has found it hard to breathe in English is that extreme density of image. If you get into it—which I did—it's fine, but it's almost too much, too thick a potion. It's less thick in Italian because there is a musicality that relieves the thickness. But in English it doesn't have that. In a way, the fragmentation on the page into lines of poetry is a way of re-infusing that musicality, within the English language. It also was fascinating to me because I suddenly saw a parallel between the decision to bring a line to an end and the cutting of the end of scene in film.

MO: I know. When I phoned you and told you how good and natural the line breaks seemed, and then to hear that you'd not done this before . . . I was amazed at that.

WM: We confront this all the time in editing: the point at which you decide to end the shot usu-

Malaparte (top) with friend

ally has very little to do with the grammar of the scene around it. You do not end a shot at the comma, so to speak. You end a shot sometimes right in the middle of a word, and go on to another shot with the dialogue hanging over. But the architecture of those shots, and where you choose to end the line, has to do with the rhythmic balance of the material up to that moment. If you let it go any longer the shot becomes overripe. You've extended it longer than it rhythmically wants to be. If you cut away too soon, it is abrupt, undeveloped, unmusical.

MO: Robert Creeley is the master at line breaks in poetry. But where he breaks the line is utterly bound up with his voice and persona—so the craft represents him, draws a portrait of him, as much as the text does. There is no abstract rule of craft one brings to the text of a poem; the form does have to somehow mirror and express the speaker's state and nature. There is a wonderful statement about Creeley by the poet Sharon Thesen that describes this. "Creeley's different. . . . when you see/hear him read it's almost like managing pain. . . . it's that probing consciousness, the turnings toward and away from what can literally be borne in or by the line. . . . and it's all IN the line. . . . his vocabulary is not large and florid. There's that intelligence that just will not exceed its form. . . . pulls back with that lovely eloquent 'humilitas' Olson liked to talk about."

In your translating and editing of Malaparte's poems such as "Sleepwalking," or for instance "The Wind," were you really faithful to the text?

WM: Yes. Well, as faithful as a translator can be. There is the Italian adage: *traduttore, traditore*—translator, betrayer.

MO: So you did at times edit the original text?

WM: Yes, but I hope I betrayed the surface only in the interests at getting at a deeper truth. In one language an idea can be expressed in a single word and in another language you need five words for it. If you translated each of those words literally, there would be something wrong. So it might be better to find out what happens if you condensed these five into a single word. And then what does that do to the architecture of the rest of the material? You probably have to make other adjustments as a result, and so on.

MO: But if you felt the length of the poem was fine, but thought that two of the stanzas, to do with the blind horse and the dog, seemed too much, within the context of the poem, would you have taken them out?

WM: Yes, I would. In fact, "The Wind" exists on its own as a chapter within a book. "Sleepwalking" is a theme in the first chapter of a book that has other themes entwined within it, which I teased apart. "Sleepwalking" was from an unfinished book that was published after Malaparte's death. What I did was extract the sleepwalking story from a larger context and give it a shape that allowed it to stand on its own.

MO: Has that book been translated?

WM: No.

MO: What surprised me also, and I didn't know if this was you or Malaparte or both of you, was the humour. In "Today We Fly," the description of the motor of a small plane that is like a buzzing fly. . . . Was that you?

WM: No, it's him. He's full of that. But you have to be alive to it. It's subtle—particularly for an American audience—so far from overt that it's easy to miss it unless you're alive to it. I find his work is infused with this quality. . . . There's a wonderful dinner in *The Skin*, that takes place just before the Allies move into Rome. He's serving as an aide-de-camp with the French army, and they've made camp on the hills looking out over Rome. Some French generals and Moroccan soldiers are having *couscous* for dinner. During the preparations for dinner there's an explosion—a grenade goes off in the background—and one of the Moroccans loses a hand. During the dinner the subject of Malaparte's experiences in his book *Kaputt* comes up, and one of the French generals protests, "Why do these incredible things happen to you, Malaparte? I'm a general and I've gone through the whole war and nothing incredible ever happened to me. You must be inventing these things." And Malaparte says, "No I don't invent them. I may be a magnet for them. But they happen."

There's a debate back and forth and then Malaparte says, "Well, in fact, as I've been talking to you the most incredible thing has happened, just as we've been sitting here."

"What is it?"

He says, "Well, as I was eating my food I discovered in my *couscous* some human fingers mixed in with the meal. Naturally, being a good guest, I didn't mention this and have been eating as if it was really prepared for me." Everyone else at the table goes into a state of shock, and he says, "No, no, look. You can see these little bones on the plate. What must have happened was that the Moroccan's hand landed in the kettle in which the lamb stew was being pre-pared and it was cooked along with the lamb stew and served to me."

They're all revolted, but one of the guests, Jack, an American friend of Malaparte's, examines the plate and realizes that he's played a joke—that it's just lamb bones carefully arranged to look like a hand. After the dinner, Jack is slapping Malaparte on the back and saying, "What a jokester! What a trickster!" Yet, with this mixture of the true and the concocted, Malaparte ends the story on a note of ambiguity. It's finally unclear whether it was a human hand or not. And perhaps the joke was on Jack, after all. But it's funny. And horrible. In his introduction to *Kaputt* he writes: "this is a gay and gruesome book."

Generally speaking, the only accounts of the war experience from the Fascist side came either from non-literary people or from the Nazis themselves and you had to discount what they said because they were Nazis. Whereas here was Malaparte, this much more neutral, ironic observer, telling you things you hadn't heard before, and in that particular way of his. That's what I responded to, I guess.

MO: I remember a story about William Carlos Williams visiting Ford Madox Ford in France. They're walking in a field and Ford is expounding on his theories of Impressionism and the Modern Novel and so forth. In his journals, Williams wrote: "For forty minutes Ford was going on and he didn't even notice that nearby there was a sparrow, terrified because we were approaching its nest." A magazine ran Williams's account on the left-hand page, and on the opposite page they ran Ford's diary account of the same afternoon. And Ford's entry was al-most entirely about that sparrow he saw on the walk. It wasn't anything to do with aesthetics. It was wonderful, full of details, his mind was totally on the three little birds in their nest.

Sleepwalking

CURZIO MALAPARTE

In the late 1940's, when his mother was dying, Malaparte returned to Tuscany,
a part of Italy he had visited only infrequently since he ran away from home in 1914
(aged sixteen) to fight with the Légion Garibaldienne *in France.*

So this is my native country,
the land where I was born a foreigner,
the home where I came to know the loneliness
of the outsider, the solitude
of hope, the struggles
of becoming a man.

And it was here I died,
that first time, and descended
to the streets of that other country,
the country of the dead,
and lifting my eyes I saw rivers
flowing through the sky, and the roots of trees
hanging like brown forests
in the vaulted ground above my head.

I saw animals before they were animals:
white shadows, already warm, and running,

eager to become horses, dogs,
sheep, and cattle.
And I saw the shadows of people
newly dead:
white shadows, already cold,
and lying still.

The landscape above was so delicate
that even a casual glance
could pry open the tender canvas
of its hills, trees, and walls,
revealing that mysterious country beneath,
crowded with the ghosts of trees,
the white ghosts of trees, houses, animals, and stones,
of horses, dogs, and sheep.
Crowded, too, with the ghosts of men and women,
white ghosts from the canvasses of Filippino Lippi,
Sandro Botticelli, and Leonardo.

After many years, I had returned
to face that world forbidden to me for so long,
the secret country of my childhood,
traversed so many times with Edo,
months after he had died, poor Edo,
pale and delicate,
with his sad and affectionate voice.

To confront that time of my childhood
when I would slip naked from my bed
and sleepwalk through the night
between Santa Lucia and Le Sacco,
impelled by some deep fever.

My brother Sandro had shown me the way.
I would watch him slide from beneath the covers

and venture out into the yard, asleep,
open the gate at the bottom of the garden
and wander through the priest's orchard
and the Mannocci farm, still asleep,
toward Le Sacca.
But he would always return before dawn,
slipping silently back into bed,
perspiring, oblivious.

One night he reached for my hand
and we left the house together
to roam through the countryside, asleep
in the warm nights of spring,
each night for many nights.

Then he fell sick.
And when he was cured,
he was also cured of his habit.
But I continued, alone,
and he would now follow at a distance
to make sure that nothing befell me,
afraid that I might wake suddenly
in the middle of a field.

Every morning I would find myself back in bed,
exhausted, fevered, cold and wet,
with only a vague memory of the night,
as of a marvellous voyage,
indistinct and remote.

The families in the neighboring farms
were told about me,
warned not to be taken by surprise.
For they went out often to hunt for the dead,

whom they found wandering through the fields at night,
sometimes approaching the houses,
crouching down near the door
making strange, sweet, piping lamentations.

Certainly I must have wandered
with those pallid nocturnal larvae,
with Edo, and with a nephew of the Benelli family,
a tobacconist from Santa Lucia
who killed himself with a pistol to the heart
on his sixteenth birthday.

And it is certain that I learned from them
all the marvellous things that fill my books,
secrets which are known only to the dead.
Certainly I learned from them
my way of looking at a landscape,
a tree, a house, an animal, a stone.
And certainly I learned from them
those hidden tongues of nature:
the languages of inanimate things
as well as the animate;
the speech of stones, trees, reeds, water:
speech more poetic than ours,
more serene, pure, and harmonious.

I would wander also with the dogs
who had been my companions while they were alive.
And sometimes with a ghost from Filettole,
a tailor who had been stabbed to death
behind del Gatti's bakery.
He was small and thin,
pale, with deep black eyes,
and he walked a little stooped,
still holding the knife wounds in his stomach.

We would amble up towards Le Sacca,
passing by the villa Fossombroni,
and from there we would walk along the Bardena
as it flowed through the pine forest of Monteferrato,
down towards Figline and Galceti.

Edo would hold my hand,
and every so often he would turn to look at me,
smiling, and talk in his thin, strained voice
about the sadnesses of his life
up there, in the world, where the word *life*
held no meaning for him,
unless it was one of memory and remorse.
It was from Edo that I learned to face certain facts
about life and death,
and not to fear the dead:
I, who had always had such a profound,
inexplicable fear of death.

But those nightly journeys also left me with a
bitter residue
of suspicion, as well as an affectionate pity
for those who lived above ground,
for their sadnesses, for their cruelty,
for their obstinacy in making others suffer,
as well as themselves.
More than anything I was left with a hatred of all power,
all glory, all vanity.

It finally reached the point that my parents
locked me in my room
and laced me to the bed at night,
forbidding me to follow the beckoning voices
of Edo, and the dogs, and Benelli,

and the neighing of the blind horse from Cecchi's farm,
suffocated by sulphuric acid.

But when I became restless in my sleep
my brother Sandro would understand,
and shake me gently,
without waking me,
untie the laces,
open the door to our room,
and follow me outside at a distance
through the moonlit countryside.

Then, one night, my fever ended.
Ended as suddenly as it began:
a hunter, some cousin of Cecchi's,
surprised me walking through the trees
as he was returning home at dawn.
He was afraid,
and because the living are afraid of the dead,
he shot at me.

I fell like a stone, hit in the shoulder,
and for two days hovered like Orpheus
at the threshold of that forbidden kingdom.
On the third day,
I stepped back into the world of the living,
marked by a scar which I carry still.

Everything I have since become
I owe to those friends from the other side:
to Edo, and Benelli,
to my dead dog, and the tailor from Filletole,
and to the blind horse from Cecchi's farm.

And now that I see before me, once again,
those waves of olive trees
flashing silver in the surging wind,
and catch the distant glistening of the Arno,
the Bisenzio, and the Ombrone,
the rivers of my youth,
I am filled with love,
with an ancient love for those dear, pale, dead ones
who wander beneath my feet
and rest entwined among the roots of trees,
incorrupt,
incorruptible.

— *Translated by Walter Murch*

Carole

MARNI JACKSON

It was early June. We had made arrangements to go up north for a week, to some cabins on Georgian Bay. The plan was for me to do some work, and for Carole to "lie around on the rocks." Her preferred version of chemo was to sunbathe on the whale-sized pink and grey granite of the Canadian Shield. Both of us were looking forward to escaping Toronto at the end of a long winter.

This plan was a rather gallant move on her part, because the two of us weren't especially close friends, and she was ill. Moreover, Carole was a writer, and a private one. Her world focused on writing fiction, some community work in the arts, and life with her family—her husband Layne, an actor, playwright, and theatre director, and their teenaged daughter Charlotte. But once the word was out that Carole had cancer, she seemed to want to connect with other people, and luckily I was one of them.

Carole was pointedly unmedical about her illness. A year earlier, when someone had asked how her writing was going, she alluded to "a few health problems." She had had some surgery for cancer, she said, but now everything was fine. Something abdominal, although she never said which kind. We accepted this breezy explanation, since no one could have looked healthier, or more attractive. Carole was a beauty—small, slim-boned, with dark, curly hair, an expression in her light-blue eyes both yearning and mischievous, and teeth that had a slight, sexy prominence to them. Her voice was low and pleasing, with a conspiratorial lilt that was always moving in the direction of laughter. She cut to the chase in conversation and had an edgy wit that her quiet presence didn't prepare you for. "At dinners or parties Carole never put herself forward," one of her friends observed, "but the things she said tended to stay with you."

Born in Quebec and transplanted to Ontario, Carole had a bipolar intelligence that was both passionately inside events and outside them, observing. She painted, wrote fiction, taught writing, and practised journalism. Her two novels, *Voiceover* and *In The Wings* combine deep emotion and sensual language—a rare blend in English Canadian fiction—with comic bite. Intuitive and honest, double-natured, her voice stood apart.

The C-word didn't spring easily to her lips, and for several years Carole dealt with her illness privately. She hated the idea of being identified first with the disease, and the loss of privacy that entailed. Then when she had to give up teaching and writing to concentrate on her health, she began to let people know, in a roundabout way.

Whenever Carole and I exchanged e-mails, she was crisp and journalistic about cancer—she was a reporter, after all—but in person she didn't use words like tumour, or metastasis, or chemotherapy. She hated the institutional aesthetics of cancer. I don't think it was denial; she was used to facing herself on the page. I think it was a writer's allergy to ugly language. Cancer jargon can be as aggressive and graceless as the disease itself. (When another friend, Ramiro, developed cancer, he and I agreed that the word "diarrhea" simply had to go. Too onomatapoetic. He substituted the word *cán-*

taros instead. It's part of a Spanish expression, *llover a cánteros*, meaning "to rain buckets.")

But Carole had a great deal to live for and eventually she tried everything she could afford in the medical and alternative spectra, from surgery and chemo to Gershon therapy at a Mexican clinic, and personal healers (the profession our generation graduates to after personal trainers).

Like an animal, cancer sleeps, prowls, hibernates, turns surly or placid. There were weeks when she had energy and optimism and almost no pain, and then stretches when all that changed. Layne would report that the pain sometimes kept her pacing back and forth for hours at night. Nights were the worst. Her doctors were doing the WHO analgesic-ladder thing, keeping her on Tylenol 2s and 3s as long as possible. It was the same story with my friend Ramiro, who had colon cancer. The intermediate stage of cancer, before opiates or palliative care are ushered in, is the worst for pain management. People with cancer can stall in this terrible tunnel, without knowing how to proceed. But when Carole and I spoke in June to plan our getaway, she was having a "good week" and wanted to take advantage of it. I had the laptop zipped and the car loaded with organic vegetables when Layne called.

"Carole can't go, she's in too much pain, and she's afraid of getting into trouble so far away from a hospital or help," he said. I was disappointed, but not surprised. It had seemed too miraculous to just drive away.

"We've decided to look into this place in Mexico and maybe give it a shot," Layne went on, "so we need to get going on that this week. She's so sorry not to go. She was really looking forward to this."

I unpacked the car, put the groceries back in the fridge, and looked up on the Internet the clinic they were headed for. It focused on detoxification and a nutritional regime to undo some of the damage wrought on the body by chemotherapy. The clinic looked too Christian-fundamental for my taste and it didn't bother to mention outcomes or any other sort of statistical evidence, but I hoped it would do the trick. Faith, prayer, and optimism are a cellular approach too. Most of all Carole wanted to be cared for, not moved through the cancer assembly line.

They flew to Mexico, and then back to the small Ontario town where Layne was working in a summer theatre festival. Carole began the clinic's program, which involved an expensive organic diet, total bedrest, and freshly squeezed juices every hour through the day. Carole adored food, and hated the idea of downing all that carrot pulp, but she stuck with it. An old friend moved in with them to help out—the juicing schedule alone sounded exhausting. When I spoke to Carole on the phone, she reported that she felt "amazingly tired," but hopeful that this was only a natural stage of her turnaround. I was out of the province, on vacation with my family. The next thing I knew, we were all back in Toronto, it was fall, and Carole was dying.

Layne continued to pour himself into Carole in the lightest, steadiest way possible, but he was exhausted caring for her at night and trying to run a theatre during the day. His sister Billie moved in to

help. It was time to round up a team of people to stay with her at night. Some were old friends, and many were from the theatre community. Carole did a brilliant job of reassuring her daughter that the best thing she could possibly do for her mother was to enjoy her own life as much as she could. Charlotte moved in with Carole's sister Jo-Anne, and visited every day. Then the key to the back door of the house was made available to a rotating team of five "night nurses," of whom I was one.

The first night, I went with a friend who had already been broken in. Carole's first rule was no big bedside scenes. I hadn't seen her since the spring, and Janet prepped me for how she would look. "Like a skeleton, basically, except the tumour makes her look pregnant." The illness had also metastasized through the house; the entire ground floor had been cleared out and a rented hospital bed occupied the bay window of what had been the living room.

A house with a sick person in it looks different at night. It's not just that the porch light is always on, or that one low light might shine through the drawn curtains. The whole house has a charged, altered look to it. On my first shift, I was nervous about how I would be with Carole—at the best of times she was a lie detector, and in sickness I had the superstition she would see all the way through me. I wanted not to get in the way of helping her.

Janet and I arrived about 1 a.m. and crept in the back door. Carole's red winter coat hung in the hall, with the short, dark wig she had worn flung on the rack above it. The faintly industrial hissing, breathing sound turned out to be the oxygen tank. I went into the darkened main room, heard the smallest of sighs, and then saw the silhouette of a startlingly bony arm lifted. The arm went around someone bending over Carole—Annie, the person on the early night shift, saying goodbye. It seemed a shockingly tender, ardent scene, and I stepped back, unsure how to approach.

Finally I came close, embraced her, and in recognition Carole gripped me, apologizing for her frayed, slurry voice. "It's this thing I have to use," she rasped, sounding a bit like Brando in *The Godfather* as she touched the oxygen tube in her nose. "Oh, it's so good to see you!" she exclaimed, as if at a soiree. But then she began shifting and rearranging the bedclothes, in obvious discomfort. Time for the next injection. Janet pulled the covers back, found the plastic port taped to her thigh, and stuck a needle full of morphine into it. You could see Carole brace slightly, hand on her chest, before the downward drift of the drug in her blood. Then she closed her eyes and slept.

We turned the lights off. Janet and I sat in chairs on either side of her bed for a long time. The oxygen tank hissed and sighed. It was peaceful to look across the heap of blankets and see Janet's silhouette, with her tent of long hair. Proximal silence. Easy breathing from Carole, punctuated by sudden, air-hungry sighs from time to time. I felt the same absurd sense of accomplishment that you feel getting an infant to finally surrender to sleep. Just sitting there felt like time well spent.

In fact, over the next few weeks, I became grateful that I was on the night shifts—they were longer, sometimes 1 a.m. 'til 6 a.m., but they had a calm, otherworldly feel to them. After months of pain, Carole now had a palliative care routine in place and was on enough morphine to keep her comfortable. Plus haloperidol, for the anxiety that morphine sometimes triggers, although the haloperidol seemed to only make her hallucinate.

The pain would always surface in the third hour, making her stir, like a swimmer tiring in the water. But the nights I saw her, she was lucid, often funny, and appreciative of our smallest efforts. Good company, despite how she passed her days. She was on top of her medication schedule, knew where everything could be found, and enjoyed ordering us around, then making us feel like geniuses for finding the Q-tips. Janet told me about one of her early, nervous nights when she was reaching for something on the night table and accidentally hit the remote control button for the hospital bed. Carole shot bolt upright, much to Janet's horror, and then they clutched each other and laughed. "I could have catapulted her right across the room."

Those last weeks were when I got to know Carole as intimately as I know anyone. Each person who cared for her ended up feeling the same way—it was like falling in love, you were in way too deep before you realized it. On my second visit, I felt emboldened to give her a foot massage. Her feet were swollen and felt strangely wooden, but I kneaded away, trying my best to be upbeat. "They're a good temperature," I said admiringly. "Oh yeah, I'm in great shape," Carole snorted, picking up on my nursey tone. It was hard for me to reconcile her ravaged body with her undiminished intelligence, but I got onto that one pretty fast.

Mostly, she exuded openness, a heightened sensuality, and a lover's sort of tenderness—a combination of qualities that melted everyone who cared for her. She seemed to have burned her way down through the usual resentments and fears to a light, titanium core of love—the openness to others that Buddhist teacher Stephen Levine describes in his book *Who Dies?*

"It is the direct experience of who we are that cuts the root of pain," Levine writes. "It is by entering into the vastness of being that we go beyond identification with the body and mind. We don't find ourselves so contracted about experience. Indeed, we see that it is the loss of contact with our natural spaciousness that is at the root of much of our suffering. When we start to honour our original nature, no longer is a resistance to life encouraged, a desire to keep a stiff upper lip, an unbreakableness. Instead we touch on the strength of the open heart which has room for all."

The next Saturday night, I tiptoed in. Carole exclaimed, "Oh I'm so happy to see you," and put her arms around my neck. She welcomed the fresh energy of the new shift, someone still unaffected by the room with its little vials and creams and lowered voices. Those bony arms clasping me, like a long, thin, eager infant. She was easily thrilled.

Someone had finally given her a pretty nightgown, a white cotton one with some embroidery, even though her alarmingly thin arms were now exposed. She had a weakness for fashion and feminine things, and I didn't like to see her swimming around in one of Layne's old T-shirts. Tonight she was sitting up in a chair. When she had the energy, she liked to switch from bed to chair. I hated the chair; it was stupidly designed and didn't support her at all. We swathed it in quilts and packed it with pillows but it was never quite right. By the time I arrived for my shift, she was ready to lie down again, so I got myself in position for the delicate tango-transfer to the bed. This was hard to do without either pulverizing Carole or wrecking your back. "The trick when you move her," said Janet, "is to put her down in exactly the right spot on the bed. We should really mark it with an X."

Although her doctor came regularly, and toward the very end a palliative care nurse was on duty during the night, for the rest of the team each shift became a crash course in the thousand details of caring for someone dying at home.

The dance from the chair to the bed went like this: First, remove the oxygen tube, making sure not to trample it underfoot during the move. Then have her put her pencil arms around your neck, as you count "One , two, three" and she musters her energy to stand up. Once vertical, you dance her the few paces to the bed, scoop up her white, cool legs, and lay her gently (but never gently enough) on her side. Make sure the cotton swabs are tucked behind her ears, to keep the oxygen tube from chafing, and help her get the annoying little oxygen pincer back in her nose. Fold a pillow up against her spine, and slip another between her knees, to take the pressure off those bony places. Make sure the maroon knitted slippers are on her feet, with the pink polish still growing out on the toes. Draw up the covers, which are never the right weight.

As I got her tucked up one night, I noticed that it was getting colder outside. Late September. A draft was beginning to flow off the bay window and across the top of her bed. Should we organize drapes? Or wait.

I went looking for the expensive massage lotion I had stolen from my husband and brought along the week before. Carole adored being touched, and loved the way this lotion felt. "It's so amazing when you smooth it, it just goes on and on!" she said. "It must have cost a million dollars."

A massage therapist, Jane, sometimes came during the day, and Carole took a profound comfort from these sessions. She had a touch hunger that I recognized in myself. Once I had become more adept at moving her around, I had offered to give her massages, which she was happy to accept. I think she sometimes tired of entertaining her endless round of caretakers, and hands-on stuff took care of that.

It was too cool in the room to uncover her, so I had to bend over and snake my hands up the bedclothes, which was awkward. Then there was the shock of her littleness in the bed. But I found areas of palpable tightness in her back that I could work away at. Her shoulder blades were sharp as wings, and every time she talked, the vibration of her voice passed right up through her and into my hands. After some appreciative murmuring, she became quiet. I worked away as best I could. Massage has always been my alternative career option, if the

writing caves. I did her scalp and forehead as well, pressing hard on the acupuncture points. I could tell she was right inside the massage like a landscape, like a canyon. This went on as long as my back could take it.

"Oh, I can't begin to tell you," she said when I was finished, "this was the most amazing evening in my life." Surely not, I said laughing. "Well, maybe not the most amazing, but it's up there." We were all the recipients of rapturous reviews for whatever we did for her.

The first night I came, I brought some lavender from our garden. Janet crushed the stems and Carole held them against her nose. "Exquisite," she murmured, closing her eyes and inhaling deeply, "so exquisite." She could drink a glass of ice water like someone taking notes on a vintage Burgundy. It was partly the morphine, I suppose, but it was also her ability to respond to pleasure.

At the end of her bed was a table covered in the accoutrements of palliative care—little pink spongy swabs on sticks, for moistening her lips; Vitamin E for her thinning, dry skin; eye drops when her own tear-supply waned; and other vials I never investigated. The main medications were the soon-abandoned haloperidol and the pre-measured hypodermic syringes of morphine, kept in the door of the fridge, ready to be injected into that capped port taped to her thigh. The pump that would allow Carole to self-administer the morphine came later.

The business of exposing her thigh to inject her always felt somewhat invasive and illicit, requiring that junkie tap on the needle to drive the bubbles out. The injection routine was passed on from one helper to another, like a muffin recipe. We also maintained a log, in order to keep track of the medication schedule and to pass on any helpful notes. These had a touching formality. "Carole and I passed a peaceful night" or "Carole feels bad complaining about the covers all the time but the weight of them bothers her." "Seems more comfortable on her left side today."

Once, I was moving her from armchair to bed when her strength suddenly abandoned her and she sagged. I almost dropped her on the floor. I don't have the know-how, I thought wildly. Why isn't there the same pressure on us to learn palliative care moves as there is to take driving lessons, or to learn CPR? Not everybody has a car, I thought, but we are all going to die. When the two of us finally made it to the bed, the task of shifting her into postion remained. But being sick had allowed the secret bossiness of the writer full rein. "Let's just sit and recoup for a minute," she directed me in her frayed, cottony voice, "then we can try again."

Sometimes she slept or rested in the dark, and other times we would talk to keep the night moving along. One night I was telling her how I often took her with me in my mind on walks down by the lake. I knew she loved the lake, from her summers on Wolfe Island, near Kingston. Then she asked me to talk about where I had grown up. I told her that I was born in Winnipeg and still had relatives on the prairies, but never got back there. She grew quiet then, and finally said, "Something about the prairies hurts." Her husband Layne was from Saskatchewan, I knew. "It's about unlived lives," she finally decided. "Thinking about the prairies makes

me want morphine," she murmured, in one of the only times I ever heard her name the drug.

It was always easy to take her places in her mind by describing them in detail. It was partly her dreamy morphine state, but her mind was also hungry for new experience and beauty. I told her about ice-boating with my brother on Lake Ontario when I was growing up, flying across the frozen bay on a homemade pontoon fixed onto skateblades, which she loved. "How wonderful!" she cried.

Another time, sitting in the chair, she confessed that she sometimes saw visions, and that they bothered her. "Like being pulled down into my grave," she said, gesturing toward her bed. I held her and she touched my face very, very gently, like a lover, and said, "I don't know what comes next, what do you think comes next?"

She was also hardheaded about moving through a mental list of messages that she wanted to deliver to people in her life. Some were responses to the cards and letters and stories that poured in. One friend wrote about a time when they had been going down a river in canoes. Then they tied up the canoes and just lay in the water on their backs, letting the current carry them along under trees. I could see her going right back there on that river. Another time, she remembered that she had things to tell me, hot research tips on the subject of pain. "The secret is not to dwell on it," she said. "As soon as you start dwelling on it and letting negative thoughts take over, the pain only gets worse." This was not a scoop, but what I did notice was that she rarely used the word pain, and couldn't bring herself to say death, either. She used other phrases. "If I lie on my side too long, I get into trouble," she would say. "How long did I sleep?" she would ask when she woke up, and then when we told her, she would be disappointed. "Only that much?"

Another time she was sitting up while I was in the kitchen, resorting to a hammer to break a chunk of ice into chips, and I heard her say, "Oh, I hate that," "What," I said, coming back into the room, thinking the noise of the hammering was bothering her. "I just thought to myself that I was sitting here in my deathbed chair. I hate it when those words come up. Why do they come up like that?" "Maybe because those words go together sometimes," I said. Death, bed. Bed, chair. "Anyway," I said, "right now you're in your sitting-up-living-room chair". "That's right," she said, "I am."

It was amazingly easy to call forth endearments. I don't know where this came from, since we weren't old friends. What we really had was a potential friendship, and a long, subterranean connection as fellow journalists, and mothers of teenagers. We had a lot in common, which no doubt had kept us slightly wary of each other. Two writers. She still had a great deal of pride about letting other people see her like this, weakened and defenceless—especially other healthy, successful writers. There were people she cared for she wasn't prepare to see. It was too hard to be plucky around someone embodying the way life might have turned out for her.

She told everyone who helped take care of her that she loved them, and that was certainly how it felt. There was a sense of intimacy and lightness in her presence—nothing oppressive or confining.

This connection made me sad for the overlooked potential in every friendship or relationship to go that deep. It's always there, it seems.

For a while I was obsessed with improving her pillows and bolster system—the bed always seemed ramshackle and lumpy, despite our best efforts. I went out and bought assorted baby pillows and bits of foam rubber to try to rig up something more comfortable. The room began to fill with stuffed and quilted things. "Please tell Marni not to bring any more pillows," Layne finally said to Janet. I had a strong urge to invent a whole new set of palliative accessories, in luxurious fabrics.

Small and thin to begin with, Carole, in a matter of weeks, became as insubstantial as a milkweed. During the day, her doctor, a priest, and palliative care people came round. The "final stage" brochures were now lying on the kitchen table. The sight of the brochures caught me offguard.

On the night before she died, I looked at her for a long time as she breathed raggedly, that irregular pattern known as "Cheynes-Stokes," an appropriately strangled term. I wanted badly to sketch her. Everything about her was fleeting and in its own way beautiful, as with a newborn. I was amazed at the changes that had been taking place in her every day, almost every hour, like the blooming of a flower in reverse. She was now becoming elemental. But there was no paper around to draw on, no camera. Was it strange to want to take a picture of her?

Her mouth was drawn back in an O around her teeth, her eyes were neither open nor closed, her skin was now whitish-yellow, and her dark curly hair, which had grown in after the chemo, had lost the lustre it had had even the week before. There was that mottling they warn you about in the brochures, as the circulation slows and the blood pools. She moaned with almost every breath, but it seemed more sigh-like than a suffering sound. What I noticed was her ebbing presence. It felt as if she were half in the room, half not. Now and then she fiddled with her blankets, or lifted her arm to scratch at one spot on her neck. Sometimes she twirled a lock of hair. The gestures were a shock, because when she was still she looked so gone.

I went back home to bed at 6 a.m. I didn't sleep. The next day I felt snagged, anxious, and distracted. Part of it was worry that I might be the only one there when Carole died. Which would be fine, but hardly appropriate. I called an old friend, long distance, but she wasn't there and in the evening I was upset that both my son and husband happened to be out. I wanted everybody home and accounted for.

On the last night that I was there, she spent about three hours in quiet sleep. I held her hand a few times and went in and out of the room. It didn't feel so imperative to be beside her anymore. Layne, exhausted from another long day's watch, was asleep upstairs, and across the hall his sister was asleep as well. Gloria the palliative nurse, a big placid spot of darkness in the chair, sat beside Carole's bed. Ultra calm and very religious, she had a lot of years behind her of sitting up with people dying. A few nights before, Gloria had sung a hymn to Carole, which Carole had quite enjoyed. "Get Layne and sing it again!" Carole insisted. The hymn triggered a dying moment, and everyone gathered around the bed. But it passed. False alarm. Hymns will do that. "Well, I guess I'll have to try living again," Carole had said apologetically.

I stretched out in the TV room, nervous, not knowing what to expect. I kept listening for that ragged intake of breath from the next room, or for the sound not to come. Time passed very slowly. At 6 a.m., I woke Layne up, and we talked a bit. He said the previous day had been especially rough. They had had to give her anti-spasmodic drugs. There was a lot of agitation (which can be the result of stepped-up, "end-stage" levels of morphine), then periods of quiet, then more struggle. "It's like false labour," one of the team members said, "and we're the midwives."

I remember how, after my good shift with her the week before, I had come home feeling absolutely impregnated with her—the kind of cell-deep possession you feel after sex. I lay there in bed with my hands folded over the blankets in her gesture, moving in the same slow way. It was a very odd feeling of being inhabited by someone. She slips into other people easily, I thought, like the heroine of *In The Wings* who always says "I love you" recklessly early. Someone open to seduction by the world. Of course, everybody who spends time with her is dancing with morphine too. So we moved through the days in a slightly altered state.

All the clichés about the privilege of caring for the dying turned out in Carole's case to be true. Being able to see her, touch her, and care for her during her last weeks felt like a great gift, rather than a loss. It can sometimes get confusing, sorting out the drama and the intimacy from the fact that the story is not going to turn out happily, at all. There is a bubble of happiness in the middle of the sadness—the joy of a pure connection with someone else's life. It happens so rarely, and only in sex, love, or death.

The women who cared for Carole were a mixed bunch of new and old friends. The only time we saw each other all at once, in the daylight, was after Carole's funeral, when we went out for a drink. That was when it struck me that everyone, not just the actors, had low, soft voices, which Carole had too - a melodious voice with a subversive lift in it, the equivalent of a lifted brow.

The night after my last shift, Layne called and left a message, telling me that Carole had died. He had been with her all afternoon, telling her once again how much he loved her and was grateful for the time he had spent with her, right to the end. It was hard to know if she took it in, but he talked to her anyway. "Then I stepped out of the room for a minute and when I came back, she was gone." Apparently, this is often the case—the need on the part of the dying to slip away when there is no one present in the room to disappoint. Layne's message on the tape was such an outpouring of love, such a selfless witness to Carole, that for weeks I couldn't bring myself to erase it.

For a while after her death, whenever I went to sleep, I would get images of her mouth, drawn back from her teeth, which were so central to her beauty, a kind of prow to her face. I would remember a persistent, delicate gesture she had with a bunched-up kleenex, touching the edges of her lips. I was imprinted.

Being cared for at home by her family, with her pain more or less under control, allowed Carole to shine as a person in her dying. It was a bravura performance—not an act, but a projection of spirit, which all great performances tend to be. She demonstrated dying to all of us around her with honesty, wit, and courage. Of course courage is the word you always hear in the same sentence with the word cancer. But in her case it was exactly that; a delicate bravery, which characterized her writing as well.

Which is not to say that opiates provided her with a smooth, angel-with-folded-hands ride. Dying still looked to me like a case of getting through a tight, scary bottleneck—a bony birth. No one gets to practise it. Do you look behind you, or straight ahead? Try to shut down, or open up? Some drugs helped, and others didn't. Anxiety and fear often overwhelmed her. But the morphine let her concentrate on something other than pain. It also gave the people around her a chance to receive her gifts, and see her light.

Incubus of
the Forlorn

FANNY HOWE

Thomas Hardy, who might be called "an incubus of the forlorn" after one
of his own characters, and for whom the past is an obscure and heavy
presence that folds each person into a path determined by probabilities
and failures, suffered at the hands of his memories.

He might have wanted to purge them when he sat down to write. But he
wrote, as all novelists do, backwards, in the body of a character entering
the story with as much uncertainty as its author, and as if he had never
been anywhere before.

Maybe Hardy meant it when he called his novels "imperfect little dramas of country life and passions." In them, he said he endeavoured "to give shape and coherence to a series of seemings, or personal impressions." The word "seemings" rings a bell.

Seeming is a word applied to chance—what seems to be a chance occasion is an event that is only partially traceable through a larger evaporating scheme.
A chance meeting is a meeting that seems to exist with a great probability of not-meeting circling around it.
As we all know, almost everything *doesn't* happen.
So the chance occurrence must actually be everything that does happen.

Hardy wrote about people failing to meet as if these failures are scandalous occasions. What didn't happen astounded him.
For some reason he wanted to know why two paths coming out of elsewhere and which converged still failed two people planning to meet there at a specific time.

Convergence—an appointment kept by two—for Hardy is the existential linchpin of his quest.
How can it happen and how can it not happen? If a person has said he will be in a certain place, shouldn't his body be as good as his word?

The fact is, once two have met, their meeting can never be erased from history.
The meeting may be minor, or major, in the emotional lives involved; but it has made an ineradicable place for itself in time.
The dread of an un-event, unwritten in time, haunted Hardy. It was a contradiction that held him inside literature—writing and history versus the unwritten in empty time. These became his subjects as much as his method.

Plot, which is twisted around the might-have-been and the how-it-was in equal measures, is any novelist's obsession.

But Hardy was rarely concerned with possibilities, which suggest a range of potential changes in fortune spread out within reach. He saw his characters as socially limited and doomed to suffer from one disappointment after another and he made it clear that people were passive in relation to history; that historical forces acted upon individual temperaments like hands on wet clay.

It was as if he were saying, too, that a writer is molded by the imaginary or that characters are the little people of literature, midgets or slaves in the circus of the author's mind.

(Sometimes I think prostitution and slavery may be the actual subjects of all fiction because of the way fiction uses up its characters.)

Without the humiliation of social conventions in any written story, there is only a protection and reification of them by the plot.

Hardy circled around the effects of convention on people again and again; *Jude the Obscure* is Hardy's final revolution and it was relentlessly tragic. (Convention, being structural, weirdly joins the unconscious in its control over human impulses. Barely acknowledged, convention makes even love-talk a defence of its governance.)

While Hardy's stories became increasingly anguished in tone, he did not escape the tradition of his approach to narrative until he renounced the form entirely.

He referred to a plot as a scheme and charted detailed outlines before he began to write. As if he wanted to beat chance and to know exactly how everyone got where they were going.

Nonetheless, he said that the characters wrote the stories, and until they took over, he was uncomfortable with the work. Their blindness became his seeing, though they remained blind.

A path is like a plot—once formed, it seems to welcome and pull you into it. A path, while it is being made, offers itself, and obstacles too.
The path of entry into a novel is tangled but irresistible; it contains itself within an ever-diminishing scheme of probabilities and projections.

Is a moment predetermined or is it the result of a series of mental miscalculations?
The difficulty of decision-making hangs in this question, and plagues the storyteller.

Usually plot is to fiction what form is to poetry. It lifts and fills the rambling language and presses it down into a single shape and sound.
If it looks as if poetry can be chance-generated, and fiction can't be, then maybe fiction is chance-generated already in an uncanny and dimly perceived way.

Characters often enter as ideas and exit as corpses.

Hardy's novels were like short stories in that they dealt with the lonely, unnoticed people in small villages around Dorset. He bore down on economics and psychology just as critically as Henry James did, but nature was his furniture and his art; it protected or exalted what was awful in the human.

––––––––––––

Hardy lived in the years when land was becoming *landscape*.
Forest, field, orchard, and small town life were rearranged in order to serve the economic needs of a few. That is, a landed bourgeoisie with ingratiating obedience to the aristocracies. These activities systematically ravaged the natural world where he grew up.

In the nineteenth century, landscape painting showed an England entirely tamed by its use-value.

The framed object (landscape) would soon become the film frame. There are—in some of Thomas Hardy's novels—the signs of his poems coming, and of the necessity for film to be born as a great art form.

Hardy's exact descriptions of the natural world around Wessex, where he grew up, are devoted to storing up images of the wilderness before it is too late. His language speaks for the trees, apples, water, birds, hills; he writes what it is to be without a human anywhere around.

He was one of the last great describers, an occupation that film would soon take over. Like Gerard Manley Hopkins, he laboured to make no distinction between words and natural things as sensual realities.
(At times his concern with specific angles of vision is a technique that also prefigures film.)
But primarily it is in the intensity of his depictions of the wild land around Wessex that his work becomes a forerunner to film.

In a sense the silence that film scores with music is the same white page that Hardy entered with words.

When a person, for the first time, picks up a movie camera and lets it roll over the surfaces, he or she confronts the intractable silence of the mouthless living.
How can you make the hills talk back? What can you do with the opacity of a filmed image?
Because words can't be there, engorging the visible with meaning, music is often introduced instead of a new literature of image.

Hardy—who declared that he was "consigned to infelicity," who could not make himself believe in or speak of God—stood with a notebook in the centre of the natural world and described it as something that experienced itself as receding, calling, maintaining, shining. A place without a person. He saw the world the way we hope that the most attentive cameraperson will see it, because then no speech or music will be necessary.

Why am I thinking of Hardy?

His men are my women, for one thing. His young male characters are
bewildered and penniless, ethical and destroyed.
So in this sense, he is one of the last of the most recent novelists whose
work I read as if they were written for me and my characters.

His absorption in the weathers of each day, the shapes of leaves and hills,
their emotional contours, reflect some similar (New England) template
buried in my brain.

Beyond that, I am at the end of a generation that began with
existentialism; that still prefers irritation to irony; and that shares a political
position sickened by the fatal incompatibilities between freedom and
equality.
(Some of us still use old words like hope, luck, labour, and timing. We are
unreconstructed but adaptable.)

We are not by any means done with the existentialism of Camus and
Sartre, and we don't see the history of culture in blocks—as modernist
one minute and post-modernist the next—but as a long struggle without
interruption.
The thinking of the fifties and sixties closed down like an old department
store, abruptly and inexplicably, to make room for European cultural
theory that entered with shiploads of prosperity and gloss.
But the same historical activity continued, following a centuries-old set of
truths: absolute power corrupts, and involuntary poverty corrupts if it can.

To return to Thomas Hardy is to glimpse a phantom prophet of the coming war world that I grew up in.

The tenacious thrust of his novels, which one after another nailed down
free spirited characters onto the fates of their social bodies, still explains
why the words "struggle" and "injustice" are knotted into economics.

His books are the close histories of labouring and uprooted people that support the resolutions of Marx and Engels.

Still, there is another reason why I love Thomas Hardy: because he finds no happiness in memory.
He can't execute a full-turn toward the past but is caught in one magnetic moment in time, where the eyes salt over, where what is lost is not yet radiant—not a joy but a source of deepest melancholy.

He writes as if he were ploughing a path from the wall to the gate. The future is always behind him.

Usually in his novels an idealistic labourer enters a village, perplexed and vulnerable, and develops intense desires that are invariably detoured by disappointment, missed appointments and worldly incompetence. Sometimes, there is a young woman who plays this role, and there is only one person weaker and more doomed than she, and that is her baby.

A common beginning goes like this: "One evening of late summer, before the present century had reached its thirtieth year, a young man and woman, the latter carrying a child, were approaching the large village of Weydon-Priors in Upper Wessex on foot."

Always the story seems to begin at the edge of a village, with someone either coming or going. There are, however, no margins or borders in Hardy's imagination, just as there are no "marginalized" people.
The life in the village is sufficient and central to itself.
And that centre is everywhere the character is—rambler, worker, woman, landowner, snob.

Hardy always prefers one or two characters to the others, but he is fair to them all, which creates complications for plot.
This sometimes results in one character peeking at another—not on purpose, but because of timing, an accidental glimpse that turns into a

prolonged pause.

Peeking lets Hardy be in two places at once, and dispenses more innocence on people than they would otherwise be able to demonstrate. Peeking is like watching someone sleep. It is also like looking back in time or watching a movie.

The character with whom Hardy generally identifies the most is someone who enters his story uncorrupted. The character is subjected to experience—experience being anything that occurs as an outcome of necessity. Experience is necessity. For Hardy, the rest is calculation and malign excess.

He doesn't like the middle-men or women, that great spread of settled society that sends out representatives to exploit the unsettled ones, because they are oblivious of the effects of their actions and of the reality of the people they are affecting.

In his novel *The Woodlanders* the thickening of a middle-class presence in a rural woodland village leads to a series of weak knocks, over-hearings, misunderstandings, and bad timing.

The middle people err in relation to their interest in profit. They calculate their future on the basis of their own early experience with financial difficulty. This rules them, allows them to sell their own children in the name of security.

The unstable and uprooted people err in relation to their self-doubt and lowered sense of self-worth. A chain of disappointments has given them little reason to hope for success.

———————

Probability is said to be expectation founded upon partial knowledge. It is determined by the frequency of an event occurring sequentially. Probability goes in both directions—toward past and future.

For example I will probably make it from here to the door because I have done so before.

Probability becomes increasingly complex with the introduction of other people's feelings, sex, broken hearts, empathy, someone's unpredictability, and the development of mistrust.

If you had full knowledge there would be no more probability, and you would see only a dull fractal consistency to the shapes of things and their paths.

But as it is, many people either foresee nothing but trouble ahead ("Danger—Heartbreak Ahead") or they refuse to see any trouble at all in case it will paralyze them.

(You feel yourself to be lost from sight only when you are intensely suffering. For some, blessed by obscurity.

The more blessed, the more wobbly the borders between parts, like the hair cut and sold, hair which is a thread to the ethereal.)

The walls of a woman's womb contain the weakest living body, and in Hardy's stories there is often a miscarriage, or a child who dies. This event dispels all notions of margin, or border, because the air into which the weak extras fall is an air beyond experience.

An air of unrealized probabilities and untried survival.

A baby dies under the sign of lust alone, which is a blank.

Why else did the Church assign the ghosts of babies to Limbo where all is probable and nothing extant, or tainted by having been?

The margins there are infinite. In Limbo dwell all those whom statistics leave out. Those who are not in heaven, not in hell, but somewhere hovering.

It is like a waste-field for the unexceptional, and the undeveloped, the aborted and miscarried.

What happens in and to Limbo? Does it float around us? Do its souls ever escape from the possible into the good?

One fears the worst for those in Limbo—that they are outside of all attributes, unnamed, unclaimed, pure figures as transparent as glass, with nowhere to go.

Limbo is like a section of God—an invisible weight without boundaries. It exists in the range of consciousness; it holds what has slipped away, unnoticed. Like the half-formed cherubs emerging from clouds in paintings of the Annunciation, those in Limbo look happy about nothing.

Babies died with their mothers, and alone, in large quantities until recently in the West as they continue to do around the world. They were banished to Limbo, then, where they wait for nothing, not even the Reckoning because they have come from nothing in the way of experience.

Children in Hardy's novels seem to exist as probabilities, threats either in utero or near the central story, pulling characters into poverty. The presence of a child indicates a probable decline or disaster. The carrying of a child signals destitution.

———————

One novel begins: "On an early winter afternoon, clear but not cold, when the vegetable world was a weird multitude of skeletons through whose rise the sun shone freely, a gleaming landau came to a pause on the crest of a hill in Wessex."

In 1870, Hardy noted in his journal: "Mother's notion, and also mine: that a figure stands in our van with an arm uplifted, to knock us back from any prospect we indulge in as probable."

He took notes wherever he went, using the methodology of science that was becoming popular then. But he was always mesmerized by the blocked path, the road not taken. The action never made. The ghost of the lost became increasingly actual and threatening.

As a committed agnostic, he noticed that the war between body and soul is generally won by the body, which pleased him since he was himself an erotic thinker, who generally took the woman's part. He remembered women at the same time that he saw them.

Marty South, in *The Woodlanders*, is a young spar-maker by night and apple-picker and presser by day. Her one claim to beauty is her hair—whose abundance was "almost unmanageable . . . its true shade a rare and beautiful approximation to chestnut." A man wants to buy it from her to sell to a rich woman, and Marty says, "What belongs to me I keep." He compares how much she makes at her difficult day and night jobs with what she would get for her hair, and before long, she is persuaded, and she sells her hair.

This transaction corresponds to the destruction of the orchards and woodlands in the story surrounding Marty South. The selling of part of her body—her ethereal and luminous hair—is the ultimate symbol of a person's renunciation to the profiteers moving in on the land.

If any good story should illuminate these three areas of truth—the psychological, the socio-political and the existential—then Hardy accomplishes that in several of his novels. The act of turning a page—like lifting a veil—when reading Hardy, is to participate in entering haunted, beautiful paths.
The un-manifested, the unrealized, and dis-appointed suffer in the margins and out into the space surrounding the book. They circulate unexpressed, but possibly so close to actualization as to fill the consciousness of the reader with their presence.

When a choice enters a story it enters as a tiny trap more than as an opportunity.
Once the choice is made—"written in"—it can't be read as an error but as a fate.
When the choice is influenced by casual moments—a storm, a letter blows away, or the face turns toward another; when the cruel words are uttered as easy speech or when the plan turns out to be an embarrassment—if it is now written in, it can't be written out.
None of us dares to say that a major choice we made was a mistake.
We can't quite form such a judgment without fear. Instead, there is a

retrospective accounting for all the contingencies that added up to the final selection.

Or we can do something that Hardy does.

We can see the whole sequence of events as always leading *away* from our arrival at the place where we really, originally wanted to be. We can see nothing but the absence of a progress; if anything, a circular turn, disruption, a raining down of distractions and misunderstandings.

The once-possible for a character becomes increasingly improbable.

The contradiction between the elusive and the trap is a contradiction inherent in story-writing itself.

How can something add up, when it is only conceived and then understood in reverse? By subtracting, until a lot of it is gone.

A tragic accident, for instance, means something terrible happened outside anyone's usual calculations. Even as you can go over every step that led to it, wishing you had chosen several other options during its progress—because it was never "probable"—it cannot be adequately explained backwards.

You have to cut (or add) certain passages in order to make the accident seem probable.

An accident can't be added to the account without changing everything around it to make it look inevitable.

Otherwise an accident in a plot is like a lost page. It falls out of the book as a coincidence, or an act of God or Nature—earthquake, twister, shark, volcano, car crash, fiery explosion.

It splits and empties what was moving along systematically. It isn't fair.

It is this question of fairness that haunts the pages of a story.

It is what is meant by a good plot. It is what is intended by any writer who says a story finally works.

The characters have received equal time, equal attention (not necessarily in the amount of writing ascribed to them), and have passed through a series of scenes, interacting, with respect for the community of sentences

as being both judgments and fates.
A social logic prevails. It can be read backwards and forwards seamlessly.

(But the world was unimaginably unfair in Hardy's mind.)

His skeptical novels are precursors of secular mid-twentieth century novels, perhaps the last best example of that tradition that lingered from the preceding century.
While they tell us what it was like to live in nineteenth century England and what kinds of failures and chances could redirect the course of an ordinary person's life when history imposed itself in sharp, spasmodic acts of destruction (industry), Hardy's pen is dipped in a metaphysical despair that Celine or Beckett would recognize.

His despair exceeds his subject, because it precedes it. He begins and stays at the half-turn, where, like a wounded angel, he has paused to look back and can't execute another move.
He reports on remorse. He reiterates the scene of the crime. He is mesmerized by it. A saturated landscape contains figures like the phantoms made of paint that trail across canvases.
The frame is immovable, the history closed on this "weather that the shepherd shuns."

Paradise may be the time when we can finally turn to our past and see that its beauty was there despite our being there. In fact, its beauty can finally be seen because we aren't there.

The purgatorial past is personal, it has your own smell and breath across it, and no matter how much you wish for the light to change, it stays gray and soaked in presence.
Old homes stare at you as if in a state of *unhope*.

"Spirit appears in Time, and it appears in Time just so long as it has not *grasped* its pure Notion, i.e., until it has annulled time. . . . Until Spirit has completed itself *in itself*, until it has completed itself as world-Spirit, it cannot reach its consummation as *self-conscious* Spirit." (Hegel)

Fiction is concerned with victims of history, and the writer of fiction shares their plight by wrestling with the torturous clamp of plot. So plot traps the writer with his and her victims, just as history does.
What does it mean to finish writing a book?
It means that your plot has defeated you. You have been decimated by its logic, which is finally insufferable. It has worked its spell on you. You have to end the book and get some air.

Now you can measure the consequences of a choice made on page seven with its outcome on page eighty seven, measuring it against a character's contingent and ambient relationships; measuring it against temperament, consistency of response and likelihood of the ability to choose at all; measuring it against outside forces, historical, sociological, existential—these are the ways that make the medium of fiction also the message of its content.

This is no dream, no indulgence, no sentimentality, but the study of justice—and a struggle with the cold lock of history.

Hardy late in life stopped writing fiction entirely and turned to poetry, where he continued to hover at the place where "drops on gate-bars hang in a row."

John C. Van Dyke, *The Desert* (1901)

GEOFF DYER

Even when books have disappeared from sight a trail often leads us back to them. In *America*—which I was drawn to because I liked the photo on the cover by Richard Misrach—Jean Baudrillard uses Reyner Banham's *Scenes in America Deserta* (1982) to help guide him through the deserts of southwest America. Banham's own understanding of the desert was itself shaped by his "sensational discovery" of John C. Van Dyke's *The Desert*. Banham later wrote an introduction to *Desert Cantos*, a book of photographs by Misrach, whose ongoing project has—to square these various circles—been influenced by Van Dyke.

By the time I discovered all this, the book in question had been out of print for many years. I eventually tracked down a copy in 1998 at City Lights in San Francisco and found it every bit as sensational as Banham had claimed. It was a rather quaint edition, a reproduction of the 1901 original, but the fact that it looked like an Edwardian period piece actually emphasized the freshness of its style and content. In this respect it offers a stark contrast to what, in Banham's view, is the other "twin peak" of desert writing. Despite Banham's enthusiasm, Charles M. Doughty's prose means that the modern reader finds *Travels in Arabia Deserta* stubbornly, proudly—often unreadably—archaic. Van Dyke's descriptions of "the kingdom of sun-fire" have, on the other hand, lost none of their glare and dazzle. If you read *The Desert* in the desert, you look up from Van Dyke's words and, again and again, see them vividly realized all around you.

Van Dyke was an art historian; in 1898, aged forty-two, he travelled on a pony into the Colorado desert. For the next several years, alone and often sick with fever, he wandered the deserts of California, Arizona, and Mexico. His exact route is not known and he seems to have had no fixed idea of what he was after; he simply "did the wrong thing and persisted in it month after month." The book that was to become his masterpiece was composed "at odd intervals" as he "lay against a rock or propped up in the sand." This, together with his training in the visual arts, probably accounts for the astonished immediacy of his evocation of the immense silence of the stars, his ability to fix in words the endless alterations of light as "the days glide by."

The solitary perversity of Van Dyke's undertaking cannot be overemphasized. At the time, it should be remembered, the desert was considered to have nothing to offer the civilized eye or mind. Either it was characterized by the lack of everything that made landscapes worth looking at and reflecting upon or it was imagined solely in terms of a Saharan expanse of dunes. Impatient with these assumptions ("Where and how did we gain the idea that the desert was merely a sea of sand?"), Van Dyke was the first to respond to the beauty of desolation. "The weird solitude, the great silence, the grim desolation, are the very things with which every desert wanderer eventually falls in love." More than that, he saw that what had hitherto been considered repellent—the "desolation and silence of the desert"—comprised a category of the sublime. This was, quite literally, a visionary achievement, but Van Dyke did not stop there. He sought also to advance what might now be called a psy-chology of desertness, to articulate what it is "that draws us to the boundless and the fathomless." A century on, as the tug of the geological silence of Death Valley has grown stronger and stronger, Van Dyke's speculations seem increasingly prescient. "Is then this great expanse of sand and rock the beginning of the end? Is that the way our globe shall perish?"

This post-apocalyptic quality is one reason why the desert provides the perfect environment for the annual Burning Man Festival in Nevada. Van Dyke would no doubt have been shocked to find a temporary city of twenty-five thousand people coming together in the uninhabitable playa of the Black Rock Desert, but in its way this tribal gathering is a tribute to his premonitory powers of evocation. *The Desert* was recently reissued by Johns Hopkins University Press, and at Burning Man 2001, as a centenary gesture, I contributed a copy to the Black Rock City Library (i.e., I left it out on the *playa* for someone to find, inscribed with a note asking them to do the same when they had finished with it so that as many people as possible could share this sensational and site-specific discovery). My only regret is that it didn't have a Misrach photograph on the cover: the two deserve each other.

Otherwise Than Place

DON McKAY

I keep a rubbing stone in my pocket—a piece of glossy basalt from the west coast of Vancouver Island. It's become my palm's companion, always there in moments of stress or boredom, a reassuring weight that's smoother—thanks to the continual wave action which has kept it rubbing against the other rocks on the beach—than skin. Do my fingers, at some level, sense that static energy inside the polish, some residue of the work that went into that gloss, a very local expression of immeasurable force? Its blackness, when I take it out into the light, is darkness with depth, like an eye or a black bear. Sometimes holding it I recall that pebble beach (this is, after all, partly a souvenir) with its huge driftlogs heaped against the forest by Pacific winter storms; its edge of staunch Sitka spruce backed by Douglas fir and western red cedar; its gradient of rock, from boulder (at the end protected by offshore islets) through gravel to pebble to sand. But mostly it's the outcrop rocks I remember—those raw teeth sieving the sea, constantly breaking the surf into fountains of spray or focusing it into surge channels which can concentrate a wave so that it rushes up in a spout. One stormy day I had my back turned to what I later realized was a surge channel I tried to photograph the mosaic of the beach below, and I found myself suddenly shoved, camera first, into the rock face: one casual flick from the Pacific which left me drenched.

To deliberate the connection between my introspective black companion and those outcrop rocks taking the brunt of ocean—this requires a stretch of the imagination, including what is perhaps the supreme stretch test—geologic time. I find it a bit easier when I'm back there on the beach in the middle of the forces that accomplished this transformation, but not much. But I think that stretch, and its failure, are further reasons for keeping this smooth eccentric shape in my pocket, contrasting it with the locals—those flat metal disks with their two-dimensional portraits of monarchs, moose, beavers, and loons.

Now here's a strange thing I have fallen into: when I next get back there (it's been a few years), I'm going to take this rubbing stone and toss it, as casually as I can manage, back among its fellows. I can make this boast because I've done this three times over the last fifteen years or so, selecting another to be my rubbing stone each time the one my fingers have memorized returns to anonymous rock. On the first occasion I was mostly motivated by practical considerations; having spent an hour engrossed by the individual charms of a number of stones, I realized that were I to indulge myself, I'd risk trouser-drag. But of course, once performed a few times, something ordinary gets to be habit, gets to be practice, gets to be—down the road—ritual gesture. It's no big deal, but I'm wondering, since I'm trying to think through the relation between place and wilderness without going dizzy with abstraction, why it feels right. This set of reflections is a set of runs at an answer.

Let me risk a definition. Suppose we try to define place, without using the usual humanistic terms—not home and native land, not little house on the prairie, not even the founding principle of our sense of beauty—as a function of wilderness. Try this: "place is wilderness to which history has happened." Or: "place is land to which we have occurred." This would involve asking, for example, not "what's the beach to me?" but "what am I to the beach?" Our occurence to the land—the act which makes place, place—could be a major change (homestead, development, resource extraction) or a smaller claim (prospector's stake, survey marker, plastic tape, souvenir stone), but it shifts the relation-ship; it brings the wild area into the purview of knowledge and makes it—perhaps momentarily, perhaps permanently—a category of mind. "Remember that place we found the huckleberries?"; "Well, I'll tell you where to go if you want to shoot some *real* rapids"; "Now *that's* what I call a nice piece of real estate." Place becomes place by acquiring real or imagined borders and suffering removal from anonymity. Sometimes this seems almost wholly benign. But sometimes it is possible to imagine an inner shudder, akin perhaps to that inward quailing you feel when some authority (the Vice Principal, say, or, for that matter, an author) selects *you* from out of the safe and faceless crowd in which you'd been swimming.

What interests me right now—as you can tell from my opening anecdote and boast—is the possibilities for reverse flow in a relationship that has been so thoroughly one-way. The saga of place has involved colonization, agriculture, exploitation, land use, resourcism, and development, sustainable and otherwise. "What we make," Helen Humphreys observes in her book *Anthem*, "doesn't recover

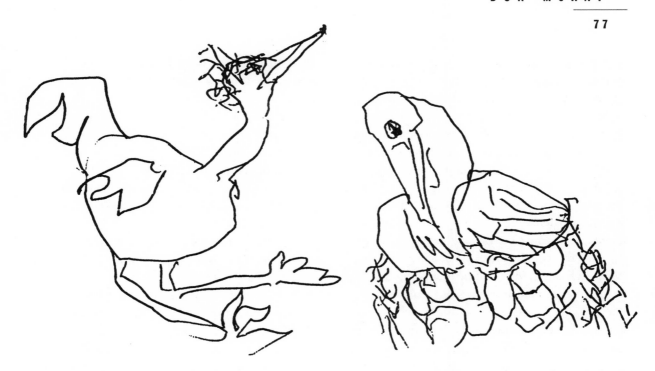

from us." I'm not proposing that we can go back, stop farming and living in cities, or undo all the conversions of wilderness to place. But I am suggesting it is good meditative medicine to contemplate otherwise than place as a routine thing. Something like a modification of the practice of fishing, from trophy hunting to meat acquisition to catch-and-release.

How about this? Porches are parts of houses where place can fray out into its other, where it can be acted upon and invaded—by pigeons, car exhaust, pollen, noise from the teenagers next door. The porch is the ear of the house. Its job is to induce "dwelling," that term in the language of real estate. Its work is first as a gerund ("dwelling is the art of living along with things"), then as a participle, then

as a verb in the active present. It reminds us—if we're not too busy firing up the barbecue—that place is first a matter of perception, then a set of activities, and only latterly walls and a roof. As John Berger points out, home is represented to the homeless not by a house but by "a practice or set of practices" by which a person creates paths in time and space.

Imagining a counter-current to the steady stream of wilderness into place is, from one perspective, to see a spatial category in temporal terms. Place is where stories happen, where undifferentiated time is given human shape, where infinity becomes history. One of our strongest and most primitive claims on land is probably the gravesite, a piece of property devoted, presumably in perpetuity, to the memory of one person, and that person's story; it becomes, literally, a plot. The marble stone on it might well be seen as an address to infinity (or eternity, its religious cousin) on behalf of historical dwelling. The body under it may be rejoining earth, but the name and the plot it comes from will live on as long as marble does. And since we seldom expose ourselves to the bewilderments of geologic time, that looks like forever. Contrary to this may be the gesture of scattering ashes, which implicitly acknowledges process and our participation in it; we join the land in its anonymity. From the vantage point of historical dwelling this goes by the name of oblivion—a name for namelessness, the condition of being unknown or forgotten—a fate to be avoided at all costs.

Perhaps fear of oblivion, of having our names perish with our bodies, goes some way to explaining those extremes of our grip on place which leave the land indelibly marked. In his book *Forests*, Robert Pogue Harrison gives a perceptive account of the opening of the Sumerian *Gilgamesh* epic. Harrison points out that the hero's motive for wishing to destroy the forest demon is to "set up his name," which for an ancient Sumerian means having it stamped in brick. Interestingly, when Gilgamesh approaches the sun god, Utu, with his proposal, Utu responds with a question like the one we asked regarding place as a function of wilderness: ". . . verily thou art, but what art thou to the 'land'?" A durable question, but not one that delays the hero in his willed destruction of the forest and accession to fame. Harrison also notes that Gilgamesh's urge for an enduring name stems from a particular vision of corpses being floated, as was the custom, down the river. This Gilgamesh relates to Utu as the foundation for his desire to clear-cut.

> "O Utu, I would enter the 'land,' be thou my ally
> I would enter the land *of the cut-down cedar*, be thou my ally."
> Utu of heaven answers him:
> ". . . verily thou art, but what art thou to the 'land'?"
> "O Utu, a word I would speak to thee, to my word thy ear,
> In my city man dies, oppressed is the heart,
> Man perishes, heavy is the heart,
> I *peered over* the wall,
> Saw the dead . . . floating on the river;
> As for me, I too will be served thus; verily 'tis so.
> Man, the tallest, cannot stretch to heaven,
> Man, the widest, cannot *cover* the earth.
> Not *(yet) have brick and stamp* brought forth the fated end,
> I would enter the 'land,' I would set up my name."

In Harrison's reading, the cut-down cedars are made to occupy the same space as the human corpses, as they float down the river in the log drive to the city. It isn't greed or the need for building materials that motivates Gilgamesh. Rather, the epic seems to be probing the darkest element in our use of the land—the urge to *lay waste*, to render the *matériel* world as matériel, to make of our capacity for destruction an enduring sign and so achieve fame. Or, as Harrison puts it:

> There is too often a deliberate rage and vengefulness at work in the assault on nature

and its species, as if one would project onto the natural world the intolerable anxieties of finitude which hold humanity hostage to death. There is a kind of childish furor that needs to create victims in order to exorcise the pathos of victimage within.

Students of the pathology of abuse will probably recognize the shape of this fury as it is expressed in families. And one may also suspect that we are seeing, in this ancient account of heroism, the foundation of the phenomenon known as male rage.

Suppose we take the idea of oblivion and try, as we did with place, to contemplate it from a vantage point outside of history. Let us consider Villon's classic statement "*Mais où sont les neiges d'antan?*"; suppose we carry this question, which is presumed to be rhetorical, in our heads, or enclosed in a slim volume in your backpack (I'm carrying the lunch, after all), while we walk the trail up to the Bow Glacier in Banff National Park. We can park at the viewpoint by Bow Lake (although it might be instructive to walk up the river from, say, Cochrane), take photos of ourselves with Mount Balfour in the background, walk around the lake, through the boulder field and across the recessional moraine, up to Bow Falls (spotting a Dipper en route? I hope so) and the foot of the glacier. These *neiges* are truly vintage *d'antan*, dating back to the Wisconsin glaciation, so we have clearly come to the right spot to re-pose Villon's question, which is now obviously not rhetorical, while we munch the trail bars. But the answers, which could begin with the lake and river we've just walked past, proliferate endlessly—not only to everything downstream (Banff, Calgary, the South Saskatchewan River, the great plains, Hudson Bay) but to that hoped-for Dipper, those glacier lilies, that boulder field, and everything touched by the water cycle as it expresses itself in the main ranges of the Rockies and eastward. Oblivion, it seems, is teeming.

For another thought experiment with oblivion, we could ask about the whereabouts of the shellfish of yesteryear ("*Mais où sont les crustacés d'antan?*") while we walk to my neighbourhood pub. One of the answers to that one might be the sidewalk under our feet, following the long temporal path which begins with an ammonoid in the Devonian and continues through the death of its organism and the deposition of its shell on the ocean floor, the eventual compacting of those fossils into limestone, the elevation of the limestone beds through shifts in continents or mountain building, the quarrying of the stone, the mixing of the cement, and finally the pouring of the concrete into this here sidewalk, right here on Fairfield Road. Once we get to the pub we can spend a few minutes sipping our Okanagan Spring lagers and contemplating the busy-ness of oblivion before—grown somewhat dizzy with it—we turn our attention to gossip and the television, on which the Mariners are leading the Indians with two out in the bottom of the eighth.

Otherwise than place, oblivion, geologic time: to contemplate any of these is to countenance our own erasures without rage or despair. I mentioned that I thought such practice good meditative medicine, an antidote to our tendency to make places into permanent memorials of ourselves, whether by monumental construction or unforgettable destruction. But I'm under no illusion that we can dwell in that moment or even rest very long in those icy waters, unless we're candidates for some version of sainthood. The possibility of that anti-humanistic extremity is probably best represented by the persona of the mad trapper who walks away from civilization, shedding all its coordinates of identity and place as he goes. I'm thinking in particular of his evocation in Patrick Lane's remarkable long poem *Winter*, where the lyric edge speaks directly to that portion of the spirit that craves oblivion, that would walk—or snowshoe—away from name and place and merge with wilderness: a pure anti-type to a hero like Gilgamesh, who made the destruction of the forest the making of his name.

> The man without a name who reversed his snowshoes and walked forward, head down, shoulders hunched. The man who climbed the mountains in the heart of winter, crossing the pass, heading west into the snow...
>
> Him walking, head down, shoulders
>   hunched, moving
> toward his own quick death, his breath
> breaking sharp and hard,
> entering,
> leaving.

What's needed is, I think, a small dose of this eros of oblivion, the capacity to think backward or forward from place to its mothering wilder-ness. That might help impede the tendency to manic ownership and keep the relationship flowing both ways. It might help us see our stories as dissolving into the infinity of details from which they are made. The inscription fades from the marble, and the marble weeps its minerals into the sea, as surely as the wind will fill those backward snowshoe tracks with snow.

What I miss most about the place I used to live in, in Lobo Township is the area north of the house, which we called the meadow—although bush-in-embryo might have been more appropiate, since I'd planted it with white pine, silver maple, cedars, and locust trees. Probably I miss it because that was the spot where the permeable membrane between place and its otherwise first became apparent to me, where home acquired a frayed edge. I'd beaten a path around its perimeter, one I still walk in memory, passing through the double row of windbreak spruce and along the drainage ditch, through some brambly blackberry canes to the weeping willows in the corner where the ditch right-angled. Beside it was a large granite boulder I fondly hoped was a glacial erratic, and around it some young spruce which screened it from the road—a natural spot to pause, reflect, and even write, sitting on the not very comfortable bench I built there. I know the kids also used it as some form of hideout at various times, but that belongs to their meadows, not mine. Our dog, Luke, also liked this spot—shady, secluded, with good access to the drainage ditch with its muskrats and the meadow with its groundhogs.

So, after he got hit by the car, we buried him close by. After that happened, I tended to pause here longer. I will always miss him; but let me tell you, that goddam dog would chase anything that moved, and he caught a fair number of them. That was the problem—his discipline was totally compromised by his speed and talent. Like everyone's, right? But let's move on. . . .

Next there was a line of old poplars where I hung a nesting box for kestrels—one of a dozen or so boxes I put up along the concession roads. It seemed quixotic at the time, more a gesture of homage to a species I loved than a useful move, until one spring, then another, kestrel families moved in. This gave everything more edge, me included. When I should have been marking papers, I spent hours instead watching the fledglings learning to fly, an accomplishment which posed for the kestrels some of the problems faced by novice skaters. They were endowed, it seemed, with falcon speed but not with the capacity to stop, so they often overflew the perch, braking too late and tumbling over the far side. (Are all beautiful things, caught at awkward moments, so comical?) Anyway, I was really *into* kestrels. I met this guy at Hawk Cliff who claimed to have trained one (although you have to wonder who trained whom) to catch pieces of steak he threw up from his barbecue. Sometimes, he said, he'd fake a throw to draw the kestrel's dive, then toss it behind him, the kestrel turning a somersault mid-dive to catch it before it hit the ground. I was hugely envious of this, and briefly considered trying something similar. But what I actually fantasized about was having a kestrel befriend me suffi-

ciently to accompany me to class when I taught "The Windhover," to show those dozy kids how inadequate language—even hyper-extended Hopkinsese—was for those exact and sudden wingbeats.

What am I getting at here? Something like this: each of these stories from the meadow which I no longer own (and which has, I'm afraid, moved in the direction of lawn rather than wilderness) gathers place while it also implicitly recognizes its loss: Luke is becoming earth, the kestrels have long since moved on. Perhaps a form of elegy is implied in all storytelling? I don't know; but I do sense that the process can be as much about letting place go as it is about making place, and ourselves, substantial.

On, then, to the locust trees—fast growing, beautifully blooming, but very fragile. When an early snow fell one autumn, they caught this unexpected weight in their leaves and bent to the ground. Many snapped. I was busy tending to the damage while Bronwen Wallace was visiting, and of course we were swapping stories. As I recollect, I was standing on a ladder with the chainsaw (bad combination, that) when Bronwen decided to tell the story about the guy who was sawing over his head when his chainsaw kicked back and embedded itself in his skull. He'd had the presence of mind not to yank it out and unplug the hole, but got himself to Emergency (walking? driving?) with the saw still in his head. True story, so she claimed. Did I finish sawing that locust? Can't recall.

So let me close by risking another pair of definitions: place is the beginning of memory, and memory is the momentary domestication of time. We could continue that walk around the meadow, pausing at the mulberries where the cedar wax- wings got drunk, the red maple beloved of orioles, and the grave of the second dog, Sam—and at each the stories would proliferate. But each would come with that temporary, provisional quality built in.

Those little walks, whether exercised *in situ* or in memory, exist on the hinge of translation between place and its otherwise, with the flow going both ways, rooting me in place while they simultane- ously open—always with that sense of danger, that pre-echo of oblivion—into wilderness.

An Interview
with W. G. Sebald

JAMES WOOD

Brick *published the following interview in its spring 1998 issue, and with the exception of the final three paragraphs of the following introduction, it is reprinted here without alteration. This conversation was part of a series called* The Writer, The Work, *hosted by the* PEN *American Center. It took place in New York City on July 10, 1997, when the only book of W. G. Sebald's in English was* The Emigrants.

Walter Benjamin said that all great works found a new genre or dissolve an old one. *The Emigrants* is such a book.

It tells the story of four men, all swept by history and internally menaced. The first, Dr. Henry Selwyn, is discovered by Sebald in 1970 in a country house near Norwich, in England. He seems to be an aristocratic hermit. He has abandoned his large house and lives primarily in a stone folly, a turret he has built in his garden. His relations with plants and animals is stronger than his relations with humans. Slowly his story emerges. He left Lithuania in 1899 and his family disembarked in London, thinking it was New York. Selwyn changed his name, married, went to Cambridge, travelled, and became a rural doctor. Dr. Selwyn, sometime after he met and told Sebald his history, shot himself dead.

The second story concerns Paul Bereyter, who taught Sebald when the author was a child. In 1984 Sebald hears that Bereyter committed suicide by lying on the local railroad tracks, and he begins to ask around about the source of his misery. He discovers that Paul Bereyter was one-quarter Jewish, that he was consequently banned from teaching—in the mid-thirties, at a time when he was just beginning—that he served in the German army during the Second World War, and that he resumed teaching. But like all of Sebald's subjects except his last, Paul Bereyter's soul began to fall victim to a wasting disease, an inner dwindling. He retired from teaching. His eyesight failed and he killed himself.

The third story is about Sebald's great-uncle, Ambros Adelwarth, who came to America in the 1920s, worked as a servant for a family, the Solomons, on Long Island, but ended up in a mental asylum in Ithaca, where he died.

The fourth story is about a painter named Max Ferber, whom Sebald met in Manchester.

Much has been said, rightly, about the extraordinary originality of the book. We may find frail precursors, possibly in Stendhal's autobiography, *The Life of Henry Brulard*, an unstable book which is adorned—as *The Emigrants* is adorned with photographs—with Stendhal's own unreliable drawings. We may find precursors in the nineteenth-century German tradition of "tales," of narrators meeting people who then recount their life histories. One thinks particularly of the Austrian writer Adalbert Stifter, whom Sebald has written about. In a more contemporary vein, Nabokov has clearly influenced Sebald. *Speak, Memory*, Nabokov's autobiography, has photographs in it, though they are captioned and reliable. But his first novel written in English, *The Real Life of Sebastian Knight*, is a fictionalized account, made to look real, of the life of a writer. This dilemma, the dilemma of fictionality at its most acute, is one of Sebald's great themes.

The fastidiousness of *The Emigrants* is remarkable, and yet it is not a dead fastidiousness. All those who read it note the patterning of certain motifs, such as gardens and gardening, or the appearance of Nabokov, direct or indirect, in each tale. The book is a great one because it forces the largest abstract questions on us, while never neglecting our hunger for the ordinary. It is full of this extraordinary, careful detail, which is part of what makes it also funny. Few people have mentioned its comedy, but surely the book does have a lugubrious comedy, and that slight tincture of vulgarity, of the sensational, which great books need if they are not to be ethereal.

One thinks, for instance, of Dr. Selwyn inviting people to dinner and giving them only seasonal vegetables from his own garden, or of Elaine, his servant, bringing food in on a portable hot-plate, which Sebald describes as "some kind of patented design dating from the thirties." Note the word "patented." A less careful writer would have omitted that word, but that word, with its ridiculous presumptions, is what makes the sentence funny. Or Mrs. Irlam, in the last story, with her English contraption, The Teas-maid, which makes tea for you in the mornings, and a photograph of which Sebald diligently reproduces as if it were an ethnographical specimen.

The photographs—some of which may not refer to the subjects of Sebald's tales—tease us as Goethe meant to tease us when he said this to Eckermann, in 1827: "What else is a novel but an unheard-of event which has actually happened?" The book's constant sense of bringing into permanent visibility something which has happened and which has disappeared, its profound meditation on the fictionality of memory and its deep comedy, all unite in a passage near the beginning of the story about Ambros Adelwarth. Sebald goes to visit his uncle Kasimir, on the Jersey beach, to find out about his great-uncle. His uncle looks at the ocean: "'I often come out here,' said Uncle Kasimir, 'it makes me feel that I am a long way away, though I never quite know from where.' Then he took a camera out of his large-check jacket, and took this picture, a print of which he sent me two years later, probably when he had finally shot the whole film, together with his gold pocket watch."

The gentle irony is so subtle. The photo of Sebald by Uncle Kasimir is reproduced, but is too dark to decipher. You look at it and you try to see Sebald in it and you cannot. It may or may not be the author. It hardly matters. The suggestion is ripe enough: the paragraph has the determination of a Renaissance still life. The sense of time slowed and mastered and then lost is given in the mention of the pocket watch. That detail of the film returned two years later, "probably when he had shot the whole film," tells us about a life, without a strong sense of self-visibility: Uncle Kasimir's is not a life with much need of photographs. Neither does Sebald have much sense of self-visibility. Yet the mastery of his book is that he palpates so much into visibility, so delicately and so beautifully.

The Emigrants was Sebald's first book to be published in English; it was swiftly followed by three further works, The Rings of Saturn, Vertigo, and Austerlitz. Tutored by The Emigrants, we began to learn how to read this strange writer, to find amidst the sublimity, melancholy, and abysmal autumn of his writing, more vulgar arts, such as comedy, slyness, even a measure of gothic suspense. Thomas Bernhard was revealed as an influence, along with Beckett. In particular, The Rings of Saturn, which folded a great deal of arcane information and storytelling into a long hike through Norfolk and

Suffolk, revealed the "English" side of Sebald (who lived in Norwich for thirty years): a writer alive to the grey frustrations and daily eccentricities of English life. One had a sense of a writer settling—insofar as Sebald could settle anywhere—into his borrowed landscape. It was enormously exciting to ponder his next experiments; no contemporary writer was less predictable.

But like Italo Svevo, who had a few years of international fame before dying after a car accident, Sebald was shortly silenced. He died in a car accident at the end of last year, at the age of fifty-eight. Along with all the more personal and selfish responses to his death, I recall saying to myself, as I looked at the bald headline of The *New York Times* ("German novelist dies"): "But he had only just got started!" As readers, we were just getting used to his magical presence. And as English readers, we were just getting used to the idea of new books by Sebald, of books as yet unwritten. And I recalled, of course, my only meeting with him: the evening on which I conducted this interview, followed by dinner, in New York. Like his writing, Sebald was calm, surreptitiously funny, erudite, and oddly pure. He was easy to warm to: handsome, fair, high-coloured (his cheeks brushed with a down of tiny blood vessels), and grief-eyed. Above all, one was struck by the eyes, which slanted downwards, and quickly became melancholy. His grey moustache acted, visu-

ally, as a kind of bourgeois correction to aesthetic preciousness; it gave him the aspect of a burgher, a solid, dependable witness. Only his heavy smoking suggested the immense nervous energy that shapes his works.

I think he enjoyed playing the melancholic German, and then surprising expectations by being funny and easy. He said that one of the elements of English life he most liked was English humor. "What's German humor like?" I asked him. "Oh, it is absolutely dreadful," he said. "Have you seen any German comedy shows on television?" I had not. "They are simply indescribable," he said, stretching the word in his long, lugubrious accent. "Simply indescribable." And then our host asked him if, given his new success, he might be lured from his old vicarage in Norwich to come to America. Perhaps he could teach at Columbia for a year, or take one of the generous fellowships at the New York Public Library. America lay at his feet. America, our host seemed to suggest, is success's real address. England . . . well, England is what everyone knows it to be—what Larkin called fulfilment's desolate attic. Sebald looked at our host, seemed to consider the idea for a minute, and then said quietly and firmly: "Oh no, I don't think so."

— *James Wood*

JW: Can I start by asking you about this question of precursors? The book's originality makes the business of searching for tracks unusually pointless and difficult. But I did want to ask you how the form, particularly with the photographs and this question of the fictional and the factual, came about.

WGS: The inclusion of pictures in the text had to do with the process of writing, which began to develop quite late in my career. As you may know, I was just an ordinary academic until not all that long ago. I gradually drifted into creative writing—as one generally calls it—in my mid-forties, out of a sense of frustration with my academic profession, I imagine, and simply because I wanted to find an escape route out of it, something I could do in the potting shed, that no one would know about.

The first prose work that I did is a text, also composed of four discrete pieces, called *Vertigo*, but could also mean legerdemain. It has in it a chapter—I think it's the first, if I remember correctly—precisely about Stendhal, and includes some of those drawings from *La Vie de Henry Brulard* that you have mentioned. The process of writing, as I drifted into it, was in many instances occasioned by pictures that happened to come my way, that I stared at for long periods of time and that seemed to contain some enigmatic elements that I wanted to tease out. So they did form the instigation for trying to write this kind of thing. Because of that, they have kept their place. It eventually became some sort of habit, of including these pic-

tures. I think they do tell their own story within the prose narrative and do establish a second level of discourse that is mute. It would be an ambition of mine to produce the kind of prose which has a degree of mutedness about it. The photographs do, in a sense, help you along this route.

JW: A banal but unavoidable question is—to get it out of the way—to ask you roughly what proportion of those photographs refer to their subjects.

WGS: This question is one that I am asked quite frequently. A very large percentage of those photographs are what you would describe as authentic, i.e., they really did come out of the photo albums of the people described in those texts and are a direct testimony of the fact that these people did exist in that particular shape and form. A small number—I imagine it must be in the region of 10%—are pictures, photographs, postcards, travel documents, that kind of thing, which I had used from other sources. They are, I think, to a very large extent documentary.

JW: By way of concentrating on one story and giving a sense of how you discovered, manipulated, and crafted the material, perhaps I could ask you very loosely about the first story, Dr. Henry Selwyn—how that came to you, how you elicited information, and then the process of shaping it.

WGS: The Henry Selwyn story is the first one in the book and it's the shortest one. That is an indication of the fact that it was very difficult for me, afterwards, after this man had taken his life, to go back to the family and ask probing questions. It was also difficult because Henry Selwyn and his wife lived very largely separate lives. Hence it would have been extremely difficult to go back to her and sound her out about the motives that might have led her estranged husband to do what he did.

The information which is offered in the story is actually very sparse, in this particular case, and is no more than I actually obtained from him during the time when he was still alive. I would probably have been unable to decipher the truth behind his decision to take his life, if he had not, at a very late stage in that life, volunteered, as it were, in a very short conversation that we had after we moved out of his house, to tell me about his childhood in Lithuania and his emigration to England. It was only because I had this fragmentary piece of information that I could reconstruct very large gaps in between what presumably this particular trajectory was all about. But as the story is described, with all its gaps and elisions, it is very much like I experienced it.

JW: In some senses the fragmentariness of the information is useful to you fictionally. One of the uncanninesses of the book is that, while at one level there are obvious reasons for this kind of despair and inner dwindling that I spoke about, at another there's something mysterious about what exactly prompts this.

WGS: The four people whose lives are described in those texts are people who escaped the direct impact of persecution, whom one would count amongst those whom Primo Levi called *i salvati* as opposed to *i sommersi*. What particularly interested me, as I began to think about these lives, was the time delay between a vicariously experienced catastrophe and the point at which it overtook these people, very late in life, i.e., the phenomenon of old age, suicide, and the way in which these kinds of drastic decisions are triggered by things that lie way back in time. The mentality of people who are approaching old age— and I think this is something that most people do experience—the fact that the older you get the more the passage of time between your present age and your childhood or youth begins to shrink somehow. You see things that are very distant with extreme clarity, very highly exposed, whereas things that happened two or three months ago somehow vanish. It's this re-creation of the past, in the minds of those people, that was something that interested me, beyond the immediate cause that led them to take their lives.

JW: This re-creation, as your book constantly suggests, is the activity of memory but is also like the business of making fiction. It's imaginative, it's open to strange appropriations and errors and so on. This particular fictional form, even without the photographs, is likely to raise the question of what is imagined and what is recalled. For instance, when Paul Bereyter's friend is describing the loss of Paul's eyesight, you write, "he contemplated the mouse-grey world (his word) before him." As you're reading that you think, it seems fifty-fifty whether it is in fact his word or your word. I'm not interested in whose word it is, but something about this fictional form, the form of quasi-documentary, automatically raises the question, I think.

WGS: I think any form of fiction does that to a certain extent. It leaves you always unclear as to how much was invented, how much refers in the text to real people, real incidents in time. The classic case of this I think are in the novels of Thomas Mann, which outraged all those who thought they had been portrayed in them, unkindly. To a certain extent I think this is always there.

But what I'm trying, fairly consciously beyond that, is to precisely point up that sense of uncertainty between fact and fiction, because I do think that we largely delude ourselves with the knowledge that we think we possess, that we make it up as we go along, that we make it fit our desires and anxieties and that we invent a straight line of a trail in order to calm ourselves down. So this whole process of narrating something which has a kind of reassuring quality to it is called into question. That uncertainty which the narrator has about his own trade is then, as I

hope, imparted to the reader who will, or ought to, feel a similar sense of irritation about these matters. I think that fiction writing, which does not acknowledge the uncertainty of the narrator himself, is a form of imposture and which I find very, very difficult to take. Any form of authorial writing, where the narrator sets himself up as stagehand and director and judge and executor in a text, I find somehow unacceptable. I cannot bear to read books of this kind.

JW: Does this aversion have anything to do with contemporary notions that this sort of omniscience, a Jane Austenesque omniscience, is not possible, for whatever reason, in our secularized world? This is not, I suspect, a theoretical abstraction—it's a real unpleasantness you feel about this kind of narration?

WGS: It is an unpleasantness, and I suppose it's a question of manners. If you refer to Jane Austen, you refer to a world where there were set standards of propriety which were accepted by everyone. Given that you have a world where the rules are clear and where one knows when trespassing begins, then I think it is legitimate, within that kind of context, to be a narrator who knows what the rules are and who knows the answers to certain questions. But I think these certainties have been taken from us by the course of history, and that we do have to acknowledge our own sense of ignorance and of insufficiency in these matters and therefore to try and write accordingly.

What you say is quite correct, that it gives me an unpleasant feeling to read this kind of book and I'd much rather read autobiographical texts of a Chateaubriand or a Stendhal, that sort of thing. I much prefer *La Vie de Henry Brulard* to *La Chartreuse de Parme*, for instance. I find there is a degree of realness in it with which I can calculate. Whereas with the novels, I find we are subjected to the rules and laws of fiction to a degree which I find tedious.

JW: This is a question which your photographs force and exaggerate, because they ask us to reflect on what's imagined and recalled. But I think also an extra pathos is that they refer not only to something that has happened and that is past, but that all photographs refer to what is just about to happen, after the frame ends. Therefore, they all gesture ahead in some way. Is there some connection between that and something inherent in nostalgia, which also looks both ways, backwards and forwards? For nostalgia is utopian, an escape as well as a sentence.

WGS: Photographs are the epitome of memory or some form of reified memory. What has always struck me—not so much about the kinds of photographs that people take now in large quantities—about the older photographs, taken at the time when people had their picture taken perhaps two or three times in a lifetime, and they have something spectral about them. It seems as if the people who appear in these pictures are kind of fuzzy on the edges, very much like ghosts which you may encounter in any of those streets out there. It is that enigmatic quality which attracts me to these pictures. It's less the sense of nostalgia but that there is something utterly mysterious in old photographs, that they are almost designed to be lost, they're in an album which vanishes in an attic or in a box, and if they come to light they do accidentally, you stumble upon them. The way in which these stray pictures cross your paths, it has something at once totally coincidental and fateful about it. Then of course you begin to puzzle over them, and it's from that that much of the desire to write about them comes.

JW: I think also the peculiar poignancy of the photographs, as they are arranged in this book, is that documentation is such a fraught subject, as it relates to the Holocaust. There's an extra pathos if these photographs are telling us that the German desire to silence and end witness has been beaten. On the one hand the book tells us that, and on the other, more complicatedly, it also tells us not to look in these photographs for the life, because it isn't fully there; it's opaque and mysterious.

WGS: Yes, and there are one or two instances in the text which point to the unreliability precisely of these sources. There is in the final tale a photograph which depicts the burning of books on the Residenzplatz. One of the characters in the story says that this picture was a falsification, that the great pall of smoke that rises from the burning books was copied into the picture, subsequently, because they were unable to take a proper photograph in the evening, when this burning of books did occur. The Fascist newspaper journalists at that time chose a photograph which showed any old assembly on the

Residenzplatz and copied that pall of smoke into it. So it seems like a document but in fact it's a falsification. The character then says, this is how it began, with this kind of thing, and like this particular falsification, so everything was a falsification, from the very start. And that pulls the rug from under the narrator's business altogether, so that as a reader you might well ask, What is he on about? Why is he trying to make us believe that these pictures are real? It is this kind of strategy, of making things seem uncertain in the mind of the reader, which the narrator pursues fairly deliberately.

JW: Can I just ask you, as a step down from the more abstract questions, about the third story—great-uncle Adelwarth, and a bit along the lines of my question about Dr. Selwyn—to ask you how much of that story you already knew, how much you had to find out, and how much you had to invent?

WGS: In one sense, this was the story that con-

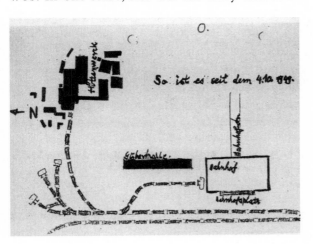

cerned me most immediately because it concerned my own family. As the opening of this particular story says, I came across this great-uncle of mine, when I was a small boy, only once, and he seemed to me even then—at any rate, in retrospect—as quite an extraordinary character who didn't fit the family mode. Then, as one does as a child or as someone who grows up, one forgets about it altogether for years on end. It was about fifteen years ago, when I came to this city, first of all to give a paper at the Goethe Institute, I took the occasion to go out to New Jersey and visit my relatives, who lived there. I looked through—as is my habit!—through the old photograph albums that my aunt had. And there was this picture of this great-uncle of mine, in Arab costume—a photograph taken in Jerusalem in 1913. It was a photograph that I had never seen before and that somehow illuminated instantly, for me, who that man was and how he came to be like he was.

I did not know at that point about the way in which he had ended, but I knew that his psychological dispositions, from looking at that picture and from the predilections that he had, were such that his own family could not acknowledge them. I took it from there. This was the starting point for exploring this particular life further. I asked my aunt to tell me as much as she knew about this particular life, and I asked my uncle, and all that is recorded in this story. Then I also travelled to some of the places which figured in their accounts. So I did go to

Deauville, for about a fortnight, and rummaged around there to see what I could find. I did not go to Jerusalem. The great-uncle and Cosmo Solomon, the young man who he looks after, travelled together in 1913 to Jerusalem, via Constantinople. If you go to present-day Jerusalem, I imagine you will find precious few traces of what Jerusalem looked like in 1913. If I had gone there in order to try and find location material, for that part of the story, I would have been led up the garden path. What I worked from in this particular case were old travelogues, going to Chateaubriand's *Itinéraire [de Paris] à Jérusalem*, of which there are many quotes in this particular passage, to travelogues written by a German geologist, in the late nineteenth century, to material of that kind.

So the text is constituted from material which comes from diverse, discrepant sources which exist at various levels, i.e., historical material, material collected personally by the narrator, and stories told to the narrator by other people.

JW: One of the things that must strike readers of this book in English is the exquisite care of the prose and of the translation. There is a tension, almost contradiction, between the elusiveness, mysteriousness, opacity of the material, and the forceful, almost fanatical extremism of the qualifying words, which reminded me of Thomas Bernhard—a kind of extremism of language going alongside this unlocatability. For instance, Paul's whole manner at that time was "extraordinarily composed," Uncle Adelwarth

had the "greatest difficulty with everyday tasks," Max Ferber remembers seeing ships in Manchester and remembers it as an "utterly incomprehensible spectacle." The language is constantly enforcing a kind of extremism, and this goes alongside something unextreme. I wanted to ask you about that. And then a larger question, about how you worked with the translator.

WGS: These qualifying words, that are introduced in almost every sentence, are certainly a tribute to Thomas Bernhard, who used what I would perhaps try to describe as periscopic writing. Everything that the narrator relates is mediated through sometimes one or two other stages, which makes for quite complicated syntactical labyrinthine structures and in one sense exonerates the narrator, because he never pretends that he knows more than is actually possible.

That extremism that you refer to is, I think, also present in Thomas Bernhard, to a much greater extent. He really indulges in hyperbole, all along. I have tried to preserve some of this, because Thomas Bernhard did mean a great deal to me, in more than one way. What that extremism to me seems to indicate is the things that do stick out in your mind, they're always superlatives, they're always exaggerations. This is what you don't forget. The telling of a tale is an exaggeration in itself. We all know that. When we tell our stories at dinner parties, and your wife can't bear to listen to that story any more . . . because every time you tell it it becomes more extreme! It becomes more

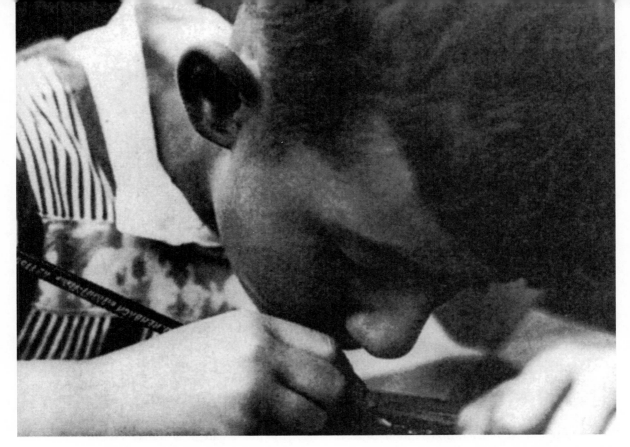

grotesque and more bizarre and funnier, or more boring as the case may be. But it is inherent, I think, in the business of storytelling—that drive towards the extreme. That invariably begs the question of what actually is the truth, because last time you told the story it wasn't like that, it was much less extreme, much less funny. If you then get a good audience reception, with a story that is untrue, and there happens to be a witness present who knows it's untrue, that puts you into a position of extreme discomfort. All of a sudden you are no longer a storyteller but you're an impostor.

It's all that sort of thing which is at the heart of fiction writing, quite generally. That is certainly there. You try to atone for that frivolity in other ways, i.e., by trying to be as faithful as you possibly can in all areas where meticulousness is possible. That tends to be very largely about objects rather than people. You never really know what these people felt but you can just possibly imagine what the mulberry tree might have meant to them, or a certain arrangement of another kind or a certain *intérieur*. It's at that level that you try to make up for your lapses, as it were, of reliability, that might otherwise be present.

Do you want me to say something about this translation business? Well, there are many reasons why German texts don't really get noticed in the Anglo-Saxon world. There is a natural gradient out of English, which is such a dominant language, into all other minor languages.

German certainly is rapidly beginning to acquire the status of a minor language, together with Italian and French. We know that the French are acutely worried about the dwindling of the presence of French on the world stage. There's a natural gradient out of those languages. Whilst the English had a very highly developed translation culture, in the nineteenth century when people like Coleridge and so on were very closely liaised with the German culture, that has largely fallen by the wayside, for historical reasons not least. It was the preposterousness of the Second Empire, it was German Fascism that reinforced the insularity of the British. In the post-war years, if it hadn't been for the émigrés, I think nothing would have got translated. All the books that did get translated into English—Heinrich Böll, Günter Grass, the early Handke—were almost all translated by one man, by Ralph Mannheim.

JW: On a different tack, I wanted to ask you—and again, unobtrusively—a little bit about your own relation to emigration and your home country.

WGS: That is quite a difficult chapter, of course. I came to live in England by some kind of historical accident. I left Germany when I was twenty-one, for the simple reason that I found it was impossible, at Freiburg University, as it then was, in the early sixties, to pursue what I was interested in.

It is something that one doesn't really understand very well now, but in the early 1960s the German departments in German universities were staffed, at the senior level at any rate, by people who had received their training in the 1930s, who had done their doctorates in the 1930s, who had very frequently not just toed the line but actively contributed, through their writing, to that culture of xenophobia which had developed from the early years of this century in that country. Of course, they had been reconstructed in the post-war years, but this past which was theirs was nevertheless present. To this day there come to light cases which are so bizarre that you can scarcely credit them. It was about a year or two ago—I don't know whether it appeared in the press here—it became public that one of the more important professors at one of the universities had invented for himself a totally new biography in the immediate post-war years, had gone to the lengths of writing a second doctorate, so that he could prove that he was another person.

That I ended up in Manchester was again rather a fluke. I knew hardly any English at the time, and I had no idea what England was like. I didn't know it was divided into a green and a black part, and I had absolutely no intimation what sort of a city Manchester might be.

I think my arrival in Manchester cast me into turmoil. It took me not a whole year but about three or four months until I had roughly found my bearings. As a very young man, Wittgenstein came to Manchester as an engineering student. This was something that I didn't know when I came to Manchester, and that I only gradually found out about.

You know how it is, when you consider your own life, and you realize fortuitously somehow that your passage through this world crossed somebody else's path. It seems to give your own life added value or significance, for some curious reason. When I first read Elias Canetti's autobiography, the first volume, which begins with this wonderful description of his transplantation from Bulgaria to Manchester, and I learned that he lived in the Palatine Road, where I had lived as well for some time, it meant something to me. I knew even then that it couldn't possibly mean something in the real sense, but it still does somehow. And this is the case also with this Wittgenstein pattern, which is a very faint one in the book, with scarcely noticeable resonances. It was initially, I think, the fact that he had been in Manchester, where I was, at roughly the same age. That also, when I thought back to that other life, of my primary school teacher, Paul Bereyter, it seemed to me uncannily similar to the time which Wittgenstein, in his misguided idealism, spent as a primary school teacher in this beastly village in upper Austria.

There's a quite extraordinary tale, where he attempted to live the life of a saint, but at the same time constantly lost his temper with these stupid peasant children, and clipped them about the ears and so on. It was coincidences of this kind, so woven into the schoolteacher's story . . . there is a faint, second Wittgenstein foil. I think

many of us find it difficult to deal with this philosophical thought, because we're all out of our depth, when we get into it, most of us are. But his private life or his person has something endlessly fascinating about it. It has so many things in it that one wants to know about that one cannot get away from it. I had the intention of doing a film script on Wittgenstein at one point, and did a rough draft for it, so it's something that may yet happen. Still, in England, I'm not at home. I consider myself as a guest in that country. But what I appreciate very much is the almost total absence in that country of any authoritarian structures.

In England, people respect privacy, scrupulously, i.e., you can leave your house in the morning in your underwear and nobody will bat an eyelid! A friend of mine once broke an ankle on the beach. There was nobody else there except an elderly English couple sitting in a car, having a cup of tea. He was desperately trying to catch their attention so that they could call an ambulance. In order to do so, he tried to make his way towards them, very much like a soldier in the battlefield. They just looked at him quizzically and didn't say anything. They just thought this is how he goes for his walk and that's fine, it's his business! Sometimes it can become a bit extreme, but generally it's a very pleasant country to live in and I'm quite glad that I'm being tolerated there.

In Burma's Guam Limbo

EDITH T. MIRANTE

Nearly a thousand refugees from Burma's military dictatorship wound up on the Pacific island of Guam, a United States territory, during the year 2000. They were taking advantage of an immigration loophole which had been intended to attract tourists. If you came from a group of Southeast Asian countries, you didn't need a visa to join the holidaymakers on Guam, who were predominantly Japanese. Burma was on the visa-free list, and word spread through the remote hills of Burma's northern frontiers that Guam was an escape route which led straight to the United States. That Burma loophole was closed in January 2001, but while it lasted, a flat fee of a couple of thousand dollars paid to a clandestine broker would pay for the Burmese passport, requisite bribery of Burmese officials, and the airline ticket to Guam.

Two thousand dollars is an enormous sum of money in impoverished Burma, nearly eight times the average yearly income, so the Guam option appealed only to the relatively well-off and the utterly desperate. The normal oppressed peasant would simply run like mad into the forest until reaching the begrudging sanctuary of a neighbouring country, usually Thailand. But northern Burma borders India and China, which are even less welcoming to refugees than is Thailand. Guam had particular appeal for the Chin ethnic group, whose mountain lands border India, which routinely forces refugees back to their fate in Burma.

When the Chins and others from Burma arrived on Guam, if they passed the airport counters of the U.S. Immigration and Naturalization Service (INS) in convincing touristic disguise, they could apply for asylum from the United States and remain at liberty on the island while their cases were processed. They had to participate in the absurd fiction that they had come there for a sun-and-sand vacation and then suddenly realized that they had "a well-founded fear of persecution" if returned to their homeland. A few made the mistake of telling the airport INS officers the true reason they'd come to Guam. Those went straight from the airport to immigration jail, where they remained until a delegation of refugee workers from Washington, D.C. came to investigate in early 2001 and got them released. Mostly, the people from Burma found apartments to cram into and lived on donations from local churches. Guam has a high unemployment rate and the refugees lacked work permits, so there wasn't much for them to do while they waited anxiously for their asylum cases to be heard and decided. The INS had very few case officers stationed on Guam, and the island lacked immigration lawyers or translators, so it was expected that the process would take months, if not years.

Burma is a multi-ethnic country which blends enchantingly the cultures and ecosystems of Southeast Asia, the Himalayas, China, and India. But since World War II it has been cursed with unresolved ethnic tensions between the largest group, the Burmans of the central plains, and other groups such as the frontier mountain Karens, Kachins, and Chins. The Burman-dominant military took over in 1962, vowing to unify Burma by force, and has torn it to pieces ever since. I first became aware of all this while living in Thailand in the early eighties my work has been to gather and disseminate information about Burma's human rights and environmental issues.

I have a special affinity for the Chins, and they for me, because I've gone to forbidden zones of India and Bangladesh to visit their representatives. When I heard about hundreds of Chins being stranded in immigration limbo on Guam, I decided to go and visit them in early 2001. After all, I reasoned, they were practically in the U.S. Having cashed in fifty thousand frequent flyer miles for a Guam ticket, I looked at the globe and realized that

they were actually practically in the Philippines— Guam was much farther away than I had thought. My plan was to interview a sample of the asylum seekers, in order to get information about conditions in their relatively inaccessible regions of Burma and write a report which might help efforts by the Washington refugee groups to speed up the process of getting them safely to the U.S. mainland.

On a March night, I landed on Guam, which is divided into:

1. a huge U.S. Navy base
2. an enclave of resort hotels and shopping centres geared toward the Japanese group-tour market
3. the rest of the island, where the indigenous Pacific people, the Chamorros, live.

The Chamorros' island, Guam, had been a colony of Spain from 1565 until U.S. annexation in 1898. Now it all looked terribly American to me, strip malls and gas stations and fast food and Kmart. I checked into the least expensive hotel I'd been able to find on the Web. It lurked in back of a Blockbuster Video store and around the corner from a Subway sandwich shop, in a rundown area of Korean-neoned massage parlors. "Rundown" seemed to characterize most of Guam, very much a spoiled tropical paradise. When I awoke in the morning, oddly un-jetlagged, and looked out the window, I realized that my hotel was right across the street from the beach.

A Chin Christian minister who had been living on Guam many years before the asylum-seeker

influx introduced me to a pair of Chin refugees who shared the tribal surname of Lal. The Lals would be my guides, drivers, and sometime translators as I circled the thirty-mile island interviewing refugees about life back in Burma. One of the Lals was a bespectacled young doctor with excellent English. Dr. Lal would pass his driver's licence test while I was there. Guam was overrun with cars. The locals were disinclined to walk, bike, or take the bus. Dr. Lal told me that the refugees from Burma had found old abandoned beater cars in the underbrush at the sides of roads and with their Burma poverty ingenuity had resurrected the cars to drive around in. The Guam traffic cops were tolerant of their licenceless condition.

The other Lal had been a pastor, back in the Chin State. Chins are overwhelmingly Christian, with every possible denomination and faction (plus a Jewish Chin sect) represented. Burma's regime, which liked to dress itself up as Buddhist, treated the Chins' religion as a particular threat. Acting in a thoroughly un-Buddhist way, the occupying army of the military dictatorship routinely persecuted and humiliated Christians, especially clergy. Pastor Lal had been jailed three times in Burma. With my tape recorder already running I asked him how he'd been treated in custody. "A number of methods of torture," he answered. "One would be, they put a plastic bag around my head, to suffocate me. Another is, they stripped me naked to be eaten by mosquitoes the whole time. They gave me meals consisting of rice and sand mixed. They literally shot at my head and somehow missed it, whether intentionally or not, the first time I was in prison. They forced me to kneel on the ground, on sharp rocks for hours, put shackles on my legs."

I could easily see through the veneer of polite gentility which covered Pastor Lal's reserves of injury and anger. He was one of the few Chins I'd meet on Guam who readily expressed frustration with INS treatment of the asylym seekers. The INS interviewers were often inept and rude. Pastor Lal told me that one had challenged an asylum applicant with, "So, you're a politician—then make a speech to convince me that democracy is a good thing." As if politicians in Burma ever got to make speeches. The INS people were not well informed about Burma, and seemed oblivious to how intimidated the refugees were, sometimes to the point of mute panic, when faced with any official authority figure.

During the next few days the Lals and I would visit one jam-packed refugee apartment after another. All were furnished in shabby cast-offs, with lots of empty floorspace for the night's bedrolls. The refugees would often feed us lunch, far too generously. At one kitchen table I met a man named Nun Uk, who had been elected to parliament in the 1990 national election, which Nobel Peace laureate Aung San Suu Kyi's National League for Democracy had won by a landslide. Like most of the winners of that election, he had been hounded and threatened. Nun Uk showed me one of his campaign flyers, which he had carefully smuggled out of Burma to use as proof of his asylum worthiness.

At the same table I also interviewed a Chin who had been an officer in the ruling army, until his reluctance to wage war against the pro-democracy side had led to his demotion to police officer and then a warning of his imminent arrest. Like the others on Guam, he had fled, one step away from prison or death. The Guam refugees were for the most part not only the victims of repression, but active, knowing participants in various efforts to subvert the regime. Some had been rebel soldiers, others student underground organizers. Many of the Chins had managed to gather information for the Chin National Front (CNF), a small but widespread guerrilla outfit, or to distribute subversive literature prepared by the CNF.

One morning I tape-recorded a young Chin woman with a biblical name, Esther. She had done some work for the CNF after she witnessed firsthand how the regime's army treated Chin civilians. She told me that her village had been burned down, and I asked her when and she said, "April 17, 1995. Early morning around 3 A.M., the Burmese military hit our village with a launcher. My cousin, the poor lady, was killed by the Burmese soldiers; her daughter was only five months old." Esther's voice quavered and tears rolled down. "Our village was completely burned and we had nothing to eat. We lived without food for three days and three nights."

Some of the refugees had fled arrest not for obviously political acts, but for things that only in Burma would be considered subversive, such as self-help projects for village women, campaigns against alcohol and narcotics abuse (as well as the usual intravenous heroin use, a plague of Valium addiction had spread through the Chin Hills), or education against HIV/AIDS infection. Burma has Asia's second highest rate of HIV/AIDS infection, and the regime keeps denying that there is a problem. Information about the disease is suppressed, especially in areas inhabited by "suspect" ethnic groups like the Chins. A man who had escaped following his attempts to work for an anti-AIDS organization told me about the shared-needle heroin injection among the jade miners in the north, and the unsafe practices even in hospitals, where "the hot water that they use to flush the needles and the syringes—they use that same hot water to do that again."

During my days on Guam, the refugees from Burma told me of their northern forests being decimated for timber sales by the regime's army, the teak and other hardwoods taken to India or China, and eventually used for American floors and boat decks. Often the villagers were made to cut their own trees for the military, as well as being enslaved for road building and carrying army supplies. Rice crops were being confiscated by the regime's troops, orchids were stripped from the forests for sale by the army, mountains and river beds were gutted and poisoned by mineral extraction. I learned of the disappearance of the ceremonial mithun (a type of large domesticated ox intrinsic to Chin culture) when a military scheme "sold all those mithuns to another country. Now there are hardly any left, and they are almost extinct. Each household used to raise the mithun. It was one of the symbols of the Chin people, and one of our wealths. We killed that animal only when we celebrate a big ceremony, as in ancient times."

As the Lals and I drove from interview apartment to interview apartment, we often drove past World War II sites—memorial parks, battlefields, or the caves inhabited by Japanese soldiers (in one case, until 1972.) Those landmarks were an appropriate backdrop to our work, as the ethnic turmoil in Burma stretched back without a break to the Second World War, when frontier nationalities like the Chins and Kachins had provided vital guerrilla assistance to the Allied cause, while the majority Burmans had, at least at first, supported the Japanese invasion as a means to get rid of the British colonists. The men who would form Burma's recalcitrant dictatorship had been trained by the Japanese secret police, which had left a legacy of brutality, torture of civilians, and the cult of obedience. In Burma itself I often felt as if I were in a World War II time warp, where the same jungle battlegrounds were being renewed with fresh blood and Glen Miller played eternally on the shortwave.

On a couple of mornings I mangaged to visit the beach across the street from my hotel before the day's interviews were to start. I'd walk past the young Japanese couples practising "Dynamic Tourism" (kayaking, jet-skiing, parasailing) to a quieter stretch where I'd comb for the beach glass I valued above shells, and wade for a while toward the coral reef. The Chins, being a far inland mountain people, had a hard time relating to the ocean and the beach, especially when I mentioned that for Americans, long-term idleness on a tropical island was actually what we aspire to. "You mean you just sit on the sand and look at the water?" Yes, I

replied, that was about it. "Oh . . . well, we'll have to try that."

The refugees didn't have very much interaction with their fellow indigenous people, the Chamorros. They marvelled at the large size of the islanders (who were serious consumers of Spam, donuts, and soda pop)—especially the tall, plump children. I told the refugees that they had something in common with the Chamorros: the old Spanish colonists had largely populated Guam with forcibly relocated inhabitants of other islands. Forced relocation, with village burning and subsequent forced labour, has for decades been one of the hallmarks of human rights abuse in Burma, which is to say, of life in Burma. The American aspects of Guam seemed to be sinking in for the refugees. The Burma apartment-dwellers had discovered the island's flea markets and garage sales as the source of dirt-cheap clothing and household needs. And one day the Lals asked me which was considered "a better restaurant," McDonald's or Denny's?

Even as the refugees became comfortable in their new American millieu, revelling in a freedom of speech and movement that most had never before experienced, they were haunted by Burma. I asked a Kachin who had been a rebel soldier and then an underground agent if Burma's regime had given any trouble to his family. It had, especially after he slipped away to Guam: "My brother was killed in July last year. Because they wanted me, but they couldn't do it to me, so they did it to my brother." Most of the asylum seekers were still very afraid that they would be sent back to Burma from

Guam. Forced repatriations happened all the time from India, Thailand, Bangladesh, and Malaysia to Burma. Why not from this strange island which was supposed to be America but then wasn't really? The local INS staff had somehow managed to fail a sizable percentage of the asylum seekers at their initial interviews, meaning that they would have to appeal their cases before a judge. This made them fear that repatriation was inevitable. "We would rather die in a plane crash over the Pacific than go back to Burma to die there," said Pastor Lal in a furious whisper.

At moments when they dared to believe that they would make it through their Guam limbo and find a safe haven on the U.S. mainland, the Chins and Kachins expressed their hopes to be settled "somewhere cold." After all, they were from the chilly Himalayan foothills of northern Burma. Guam's humid, scrubby, reef-ringed plateau was alien to them, even though the island's Christian churches had provided considerable charity. I went to a Sunday service at a Baptist church attended by hundreds of the refugees. Asked to give a speech there, I said that I thought they would be on the mainland "before too much longer." That got mistranslated as "before two months longer," which certainly cheered people up. As it would turn out, pressure in Washington (emphasizing the Christianity of the refugees) did get the INS interview process speeded up, and nearly all of the asylum seekers boarded jets to a variety of mainland locations, cold and not so cold, during the summer of 2001.

Not all of the Guam refugees were Christians, or even frontierspeople, but all were haunted in the same way. My last interview on the island was with a Burman, a Buddhist city-dweller who had participated in the 1988 student uprising and suffered through a seven-year sentence in the dungeons of Insein Prison and Myingyan Jail. With the threat of re-arrest always right over his head, the Guam route had beckoned to him. As we sat on rickety chairs in one of the island flats, this slight, baby-faced thirty-something told his story as if reliving every incarcerated moment. He told me of being beaten for singing in his cell, until he fell silent for months at a time, and faced his parents on one of their rarely allowed visits as a speechless creature, "with my shackles like a slave." He considered himself lucky because he had gotten a "health" injection only once while in prison, because the guards "first inject the AIDS persons and then the political prisoners." He told of sleeping year after year on clammy cement without blankets so that even now on tropical Guam he felt cold in his joints and felt hopelessly old. "I felt the nightmare during prison life, up to today, even though it was three years ago; I have these nightmares even now. Sometimes when I sleep I get a very bad dream—the reason why I was detained in jail. Then I wake up and I am free. I am on Guam. This happened so many times. It's maybe broken my brain while I was in jail."

As I left Guam, it occurred to me that the refugees might miss the friends with whom they'd lived in such close communal quarters on the island, when they at last would be dispersed to Michigan or Maryland or Montana. But the charm of being stuffed ten to a room in a three-bedroom apartment would have worn off. And Guam simply would never feel secure to them. On my long flight home, which included many hours of airport lay-over in Japan, I read the entirety of Melville's *Typee*, which happened to be about someone stranded on a perfectly nice Pacific island which was still not to be his home. I had been among the castaways, the mutineers, the rebels, the refugees.

Two Poems

CAROLYN FORCHÉ

Afterdeath

from the quarry of souls they come into being
supernal lights, concealed light, that which has no end

that which thought cannot attain
the going forth, the *as yet cannot be heard*

—as a flame is linked to its burning coal
to know not only what is, but the other of what is

Refuge

In the blue silo of dawn, in earth-smoke and birch copse,
where the river of hands meets the Elbe.

In the peace of your sleeping face, *mein leiben*.

We have our veiled memory of running from police
dogs through a blossoming orchard, and another

Of not escaping them. That was—ago—(a lifetime).
but now you are invisible in my arms, a soul

Acquiring speech, the body its blind light, whispering
Noli me frangere even as it is in death shattered.

We were *one in the other*. When the doves rose
at once, and our refuge became wing-light—

Christian Bök and Darren Wershler-Henry

An Interview

In the fall of 2000, Brick approached poets Christian Bök and Darren Wershler-Henry and asked them to interview each other. The two are close friends and exemplars of the avant garde scene in Canada. Their processes and their writing styles, although very different, are nonetheless inextricably linked. Christian Bök has laughingly referred to their connection as a "Vulcan mind-meld."

Darren Wershler-Henry's role as editor at Coach House Books has seen that press, and the writing it supports, undergo a rennaissance in the last five years. Although avowedly dedicated to experimentation, both writers have reputations for being supporters of the writing enterprise in general, and their circle is filled with writers and poets of all walks and genres.

This doesn't, however, mean that they value all writing equally. In a discourse about writing that has spanned many years and has taken place in many venues, they have ferociously argued for a radicalization of Canadian letters, through this discourse and the examples of their own work.

Both writers have published two books of poetry, and both continue to take vertical leaps. Wershler-Henry's latest book, the tapeworm foundry, *sends up the whole idea of writing, proposing, in a single run-on sentence, a plethora of notions, some possible, some not, that the writer without an idea might take up.*

Bök's latest is the univocal lipogram, Eunoia. *Written in five chapters of varying length, Eunoia's project is to tell a story using only one vowel per chapter. Its success in this endeavour is almost as dizzying as the idea itself; the fact that any kind of story could be told, let alone one as cogent as this, under such constraint strikes the reader as the revelation of a code. Both writers met in the fall of 2000, and from that time until now, the interview has passed back and forth between them and* Brick, *resulting in the document below. The tapeworms of language scrolling across the top and bottom of the interview are excerpts from the authors' most recent books. Wershler-Henry is at the top of the pages, Bök is below.*

— Michael Redhill

CB: Christian Bök and Darren Wershler-Henry— here we are, the Rosencrantz and Guildenstern of Canadian literature, working on an interview for our taskmasters at *Brick*.

DWH: Let me start, because this has been bothering me for awhile. I've just finished reading Friedrich Kittler's *Gramophone, Film, Typewriter.* And he argues consistently throughout the book that literature is inimical to media culture and that literature—especially poetry—does pretty much nothing except talk about its own death. This has me worried because it's applicable not only to clichéd poetic formations, but also to, perhaps, things like L=A=N=G=U=A=G=E poetry, the writing of the Kootenay School, etc. So what do you think? Are we screwed? Is there a rabbit hole that we can pull poetry out of?

CB: Poetry has no popular role to play in the mass media unless there's an actual technological change in the modes of production and distrib-

ution so that poets can control or subvert the process as they see fit.

DWH: I don't know if the argument is that poetry or literature plays a popular role in culture so much as that literariness itself has, perhaps, been exhausted, that there is nothing new to add, and not much more to do other than to stand around and watch literature crumble away entropically. And I think about things like, starting with Modernism, going from the sound poetry of Dadaism, Futurism, and Zaum all the way up to David Melnick, John Cage, Fluxus, and L=A=N=G=U=A=G=E, and even experimental noise-rock stuff, like the Boredoms— all artists who have worked with nonsense and fragments of language—plus people that we know, like Kenny Goldsmith with his "uncreative writing" or Tan Lin and Brian Kim Stefans with their differing ideas about "ambient poetry," something more like wallpaper or Muzak than entertainment. Once you've marked an outer limit for poetry, it becomes increasingly more difficult to step slightly further over the line and draw a new outer limit. And it's an asymptotic relation, you're never actually, totally at the zero point, but it gets pretty fucking close.

CB: Well, what's going to happen, say, with radio analysis, because obviously radio has had a profound effect upon the history of avant-garde literature, particularly Italian Futurism. Does Kittler go into any detail about how poetry might maintain some of its relevance in the mass media through avenues other than TV or the Internet?

DWH: Well, he talks about voice a lot, in relationship to the gramophone, arguing that the invention of the gramophone was the first time people actually transcribed the Real in the sense that, when you speak, the vibrations of your voice box produce a physical wave, which moves through the air and vibrates another physical membrane, which actually scratches a transcription of that vibration into wax. And, when you play that back, you are, in a sense, playing back the Real, and that had never happened before. So there's a rupture, but even that has been pretty thoroughly explored by Antonin Artaud, Ezra Pound and, again, the sound poets, plus the musicians from the Japanese and New York noise-scene. Even the avant-garde musicians and rock musicians that have flirted with the limits of meaning fall back into weird corners of modernism, by default, like Mike Patton from Faith No More and Mr. Bungle going back and studying Russolo and the Italian Futurists and trying to emulate that, all the way through to CCMC [the infamous Toronto avant-noise band that currently consists of Paul Dutton, John Oswald and Michael Snow]. You know, watching CCMC open up for Sonic Youth was an interesting moment because it was like watching two parallel worlds collide, you know, the moment when sound poetry could've become the entertainment of youth culture but didn't—instead what we got was grunge-rock. *laughs*

CB: Or spoken-word poetry.

DWH: Don't get me started. Enough spoken word (and here I'm using the term in reference to the Nuyorican, pseudobeat stuff rather than dub poetry, which I really like) has accreted in the pipes that we'll probably never get rid of it now . . . but all of this is old news, hash that was well settled in your Code-X jousting matches with the spoken word people in Word magazine the late 90s. Do you think anything ever comes out of those kinds of jousting matches or is it just dogma and bullshit posturing on both sides?

CB: Well, Canadian literature has often defined itself according to a stifling sense of decorum around questions of literariness. The mainstream, literary community presumes that such critical activity has little bearing upon the "craft" of writing stories, and, in a certain sense, the little microscopic fights that take place in our communities determine how we talk about the work that we produce. The fact that there is extremely limited controversy around questions that seem, in many respects, irrelevant to the on-going innovations of writing in this country is sad. I state clichés and truisms about the history of the avant-garde in my Code-X articles—issues that all modern writers have to know about their literary history, but which, modern writers, nevertheless, still regard as scandalous. I find that, in my arguments with the spoken-word poets, I feel mostly disappointed by the lack of worthy adversaries.

DWH: Yeah, it's like they used to say at Suck.com: a fish, a barrel, a smoking gun
laughs

DWH: But, I'm going to jump on something you just said, because we all know that this is a kind of nasty truth, that the term "avant-garde" has this kind of persistence—it's in our vocabulary even though we all know we're not supposed to use it (though Marjorie Perloff seems to be making a pretty strong case for its resurrection in her new book, *21st Century Modernism*). Theoretically, in a society with no center, there are no edges, so there's nothing to be "avant" of, and the militarism of the term is something that we all know is bad. I have a sign in my office that Richard Tipping, the Australian concrete poet, made, which reads: "CAUTION: There is no avant-garde—only those who have been left behind."

CB: I guess that I use the word because I'm not supposed to use it (pause). I do not see the avant-garde being at the forefront of a unitary, linear model of historical progress, but I do think that the militarized overtones of the word "avant-garde" still serve a useful purpose, insofar as the word identifies a controversial viewpoint, suggesting that we all participate in aesthetic conflicts, where certain poetic values are at stake. The decorum of Canadian literature does not draw attention to the fact that such mainstream literature regiments behaviour, insisting that certain limits of lyrical realism have to be policed and encoded. I think that perhaps a more applicable term would be something like outré-garde or …

DWH: "Avant-grad"

laughter

DWH: "I refuse to finish."

laughter

DWH: Not on those terms. Really, If I had a loonie for every critic who's presented the argument

Darren Wershler-Henry (left) and Christian Bök

that L=A=N=G=U=A=G=E poetry in particular and innovative writing in general were products of the academy, I'd actually have a bag of them that'd be heavy enough to seriously hurt them when I dropped it on their heads for making such a stupid argument. The academy isn't interested in contemporary poetry. There are isolated people, of course, but there aren't enough of them to actually change academic culture in a proactive way.

CB: I can't think of a single aesthetic movement, be it conservative or progressive, that wouldn't want to contextualize itself as being innovative, even though novelty is no longer particularly ground-breaking, since newness has itself become nothing more than an upgrade to the software of ideology.

DWH: But that puts us in an impossible position, right, because we can no longer "make it new," because that was what the modernists did. Making it new is old.

CB: Yes—

...and nothing old will ever go away again because, in the post-modern society it all exists contemporaneousl; we have no past and no future, only Gertrude Stein's "continuous present." And the question is, not only how do you make literature in that environment, but how do you live in that environment? Kenny Goldsmith says the trick now is to use information networks to "Make it Everywhere," a notion I find really attractive.

CB: How do you find alternatives to your way of life? New artworks are no less commodified than new brands of toothpaste: "new and improved, twice as many adjectives!" We have to find a new kind of commentary upon novelty itself: for example, your own book *the tapeworm foundry* does not constitute a literary artifact but is, in fact, a description of a whole series of potential, literary artifacts, some of which might or might not be realized. Your book proposes, rather than realizes, literary projects, and this activity seems to me like a commentary upon the aesthetic process itself. What does a work like yours—a book-length list of ideas for art, accompanied by an exhortation to the readers to get off their asses and create—mean nowadays, and particularly in this country, where few truly interesting writers have at their beck and call the resources and leisure necessary for them to do their work? Under such circumstances, the novelty of such a work arises out of the constraints imposed by a poverty of finance or leisure....

DWH: All writing in politically conservative society is writing under constraint, because you're trying to produce something that does not ... it's not that it doesn't have a value, but it has an arbitrary value, and that's fundamentally at odds with consumer culture because your writing one day can be worth nothing, and the next day it could be worth hundreds of thousands of dollars. I think that makes people uncomfortable. You know, it's like you spend ten years in university and come out of it with no readily indentifiable skill-set.

CB: Well, worse yet, you end up becoming not only unemployable, but also unrecognized. I am thinking of the line in your book about working as hard as you can to transform the language, but never getting famous for all your efforts. I think that, ironically, the most interesting young poets in our country have yet to find work in the academy, despite their proven merits.

DWH: ... which goes a long way toward explaining the attraction of a negative critique like Sianne Ngai's "poetics of disgust" in Jeff Derksen's Open Letter issue. Ngai's argument is that disgust is a material response, not only to capitalism and patriarchy, but also to being shut out of the canon or shut out of means of publication. If you look at the Kootenay School writers, you see that, for more than ten years, until recently, most of them had only one book, and it's not like they haven't been writing. So, I guess the question is—has the mood for such a negative poetics passed or are we in a moment where a negative critique is necessary in the same way that is was in the Dada years?

CB: I don't think that the social context for literary critique is the same.

DWH: Oh no, well, of course not, there's no World War. People aren't dying.

CB: Okay, but is it not enough merely to criticize the status quo, merely to complain about the parochialism and philistinism of Canadian literature in the hope that someday you might get to attend a dinner at the mansion of the Governor General? Do you simply replace the powers that be with your own poetic agenda? Or do you have to disavow the very principles that provide the occasion for the critique?

DWH: You've said a couple of times over the last year that if you ever had any money at all, the thing to do would be to start some sort of foundation for an alternative literary award. But, ultimately, I don't know if that would do any good—look at Kenneth J. Harvey's ReLit Award . . . I admire his energy and initiative but it's kind of a Quixotic enterprise . . .

CB: My award would be a work of performance art. I would call it "Christian Bök's Favourite Book Award"—a prize given out capriciously to whomever I wanted to award $50,000, and of course it would have to be worth more money than the Giller Prize...

laughs

CB: ...just so that people would want to win it. And I would give it to the one person who wrote the most bizarre, most radical, experiment in Canadian literature.

DWH: But I guess what I'm wondering about is the recuperability of that gesture, because as soon as you make it, Chapters/Indigo can slap a sticker on the front of the book, put a pile of fifty of them in their lobby, and they're off to the bank, right?

CB: Yeah, but at least the act would parody the protocol of such awards, declaring all awards to be the work of some crackpot endowing money to some completely undeserving person.

DWH: So it's a *Road Warrior* kind of thing. You just walk away from the tanker after it's tipped over, destroyed, fucked, and you simply don't rebuild the same destructive social machine all over again. Well, it'll be interesting to see what happens over time. I mean, we are actually starting to gain access to some of the cultural machinery . . . are we going to be able to change anything, or are we just going to repeat the mistakes of the last forty years?

CB: We are likely to repeat these mistakes, especially if we feel complacent after gaining access to these legitimizing institutions. I think that, once you acquire a little money, a little glory, you risk being satisfied with the act of recuperating from your exhaustive enterprise, when in fact, these resources provide an opportunity for further growth, giving you the freedom to take even more risks, questioning the infrastructure of culture in the hope of making it more amenable to a far more diverse variety of innovative endeavours. I am always a little disappointed to see that, once an artist achieves some success, the most radical aspects of their practise seem to dissipate at the very moment when they have an even greater opportunity to be disruptive. What do you think?

DWH: I think that the most important radical gestures that an artist makes have to do with reinventing the social—perpetuating a free and vigorous exchange of ideas, information and access to the means of publication. The thing that disappoints me the most about my various fallen literary idols is that the ones that have abandoned radical stylistics also invariably abandon their sense of commitment to the larger community: their established readership, their peers, and their protegés. I'm the editor of Coach House Books now, but I have no intention of staying there forever; it needs to be passed on to the next group of young writers to ensure that they gain the ability to publish a lot more rapidly than we did. If I overstay my welcome, please put a cap in my ass.

CB: You can count on me. *laughs.* Now that the dust has long since settled from the publication of *Nicholodeon*, a book notoriously informed by the work of bpNichol, I'm wondering how your attitude toward the legacy of Nichol has changed.

DWH: Well, I like to think of it now as the most expensive colouring book that has been produced in this country in the last five years. Just after I finished it, I had this long conversation with Bill Kennedy (the consicence of the Toronto literary community), and Bill said "Well, it's a lot like standing on the edge of a very tall cliff commenting on how far down the bottom is, isn't

it?" What Bill was trying to tell me was that there's a certain impulse for young writers to over-explain what it is that they're doing, to have this massive theoretical apparatus in place, when it's not really their job to do that—we need to spend more energy on pushing the art and less on exegesis.

There are things about *Nicholodeon* that I like, still, but in some ways it's kind of a precious book. I wanted it to crack open the existing school of Nichol criticism that's based around anecdotal discussions of the poet's life, but in some respects it seems to have abetted the Nichol cottage industry in a different direction, one that's not necessarily better. I wince every time someone sends me an e-mail about the latest bpNichol "translation" that they've done. I mean, that's nice, but I wrote Nicholodeon to work through those questions for myself, and those questions have been answered for me, and I'm not particularly interested in them anymore (I dealt with all of this in gory detail in Open Letter 11.3, Fall 2001). If you look at the book carefully, maybe less than a third of the book actually concerns Nichol in any way. I have more than a slight ambivalence around it; I guess it's a very typical first book in that respect.

CB: Now that you're one of the editors at Coach House Books, you have some unenviable responsibilities. . .

laughs

CB: . . . among them, determining the taste of future Canadian readers (laughs). And I'm just curious, what direction do you see yourself taking the press, and how does your work at the press affect your own poetry?

DWH: Well, I think it would be hubristic to say that what we're doing at Coach House will affect the taste of future readers, because people buy books, but they buy mass-market books, and what we do is on a much more humble scale. It's not financially possible for us to create books that will reach a mass audience, and even if we could, I don't think I'd want to, because the writing that I'm trying to propagate has a fairly specific audience, and many of the writers themselves don't pretend to populism in any way.

It's a hard business, running a press, and I guess on a lot of levels there are compromises about my own writing and things that I have to put aside that I would like to do to keep the press going. But it's not like, with the economy the way that it is and grants getting scarcer, that anybody will ever offer me a fully operating literary press again. Certainly not with the autonomy that I have at Coach House. So, it's kind of a historical contingency that I think I have to do this now and I have to take the opportunity to put the kinds of things that we've been talking about in print.

A lot of the books that we've put out over the last couple of years represent what I think is the best of the innovative poetry by younger writers that's been published in this country (and parts of the US) in recent memory: Dan Farrell's *The Inkblot Record*, Nancy Shaw and Catriona Strang's *Busted* damian lopes' *sensory deprivation/dream poetics*, Kenny Goldsmith's

Fidget, and your own *Eunoia*. We've also done a good job of printing and reprinting the writing that serves as context for this newer work—the first volume of Steve McCaffery's selected works received a Governor General's Award nomination; Bruce Andrews's massive *Lip Service* (his reworking of Dante's *Paradiso*) is doing really well, and we're talking about doing a big selected works for Fred Wah too. So, at least there there is an opportunity here to present an alternative. And in conjunction with books like Dorothy Lusk's *Ogress Oblige*, Lisa Robertson's *Debbie* and *The Weather*, and Marina Roy's *sign after the X*, from presses like Krupskaya, New Star, Anansi, and Arsenal Pulp, I think that it is possible to make a difference in the national literary culture. The world needs, Canada needs, another generic poetry press producing lyric verse about as badly as it needs a kick in the head. Just getting the writers I've mentioned into print is an act with aesthetic and even political implications.

The stuff that we're doing with Internet publishing, trying to convince people that they should be writing differently to address media culture is a political act. There have been a few experiments that I think are relatively successful,; damian lopes' work is a shining example of what can be done. Brian Kim Stefans' online work <www.arras.net> the things that Kenny Goldsmith has put on the Ubuweb <www.ubu.com> are also exemplary. But there's a whole education process that has to go on around that. You have to create a group of

P.M.'s & Governments of Canada.

		From	To	Years
Sir	John A Macdonald C	1867	1873	6
	ALEXANDER Mackenzie L	1873	1878	5
Sir	John A Macdonald C	1878	1891	13
Sir	John Abbott C	1891	1892	1
Sir	John Thompson C	1892	1894	2
Sir	Mackenzie Bowell C	1894	1896	2
Sir	Charles Tupper (2 MONTHS) C	1896	—	0
Sir	Wilfred Laurier L	1896	1911	15
Sir	Robert L Borden C	1911	1920	9
	Arthur Meighen C	1920	1921	1
	Wm. Mackenzie King L	1921	1926	5
	Meighen (3 MONTHS) C	1926	1920	0
	King L	1926	1930	4
	R.B. Bennett C	1930	1935	5
	King L	1935	1948	13
	Louis St Laurent L	1948	1957	9
	John Diefenbaker C	1957	1963	6
	Lester Pearson L	1963	1948	5
	Pierre L Trudeau L	1968	1979	11
	Joe Clark C	1979	1980	1
	Pierre L Trudeau L	1980		

P.M.'s Returned after defeat

J A Macdonald	1 repeat	C	
Arthur Meighen	1 "	C	
Mackenzie King	2 "	L	
Trudeau	1 "	L	
	5		

	Total	Cons	Libs
number of Governments	21 =	12	9
" " Prime Ministers	16 =	10	6
" " Parliaments — 36 32			

Years in Government:

	L	C	1867-1980
	67	46 =	113 years

1867-1900	C	L
	24	9
1900-1980	22	58
	46	67

writers who are capable of doing their own programming, which means more than transcribing poems into HTML and putting them on the Web; I'm afraid that a lot of what we're doing at Coach House is still in that category. Just adding some animated GIFs does not make for a new genre, but I'm beginning to think that maybe the website itself is a compositional unit and that there are a whole series of important principles that evolve from that. Like an online poetics might be a poetry that's based on metonymy as its central trope. It would have to be highly visual. It could incorporate bits of things from other poetry—sound poetries, concrete poetries—in order to make itself something other, and it may well be the crack in the wall that we're looking for.

CB: Web sites give us the opportunity to produce a mélange of different aesthetic genres under the umbrella of multimedia, but nobody is writing with these kinds of formalistic sensibilities; nobody is writing a book purely for the fun of seeing it experienced on the Internet. We publish books online only after the fact. The media of the past merely provides content for the media of the future.

DWH: Good online writing exceeds paper. Brian's *The Naif and the Bluebells* and *The Dreamlife of Letters* will probably never become paper books, and damian's *sensory deprivation/dream poetics* <www.chbooks.com/online/sensory_deprivation/index.html> only became one with an extreme amount of shoehorning to make it fit into paper form, because it does things that a paper book could not do and it forces you to address the metaphors of online browsing—things like 'pointing' and 'clicking'—that are already dead. You expect that, when you roll your cursor over an object on the screen that it's passive until you click on it, that it moves at your behest. *sensory deprivation/dream poetics* does the opposite; it works on subtractive principles, so that as soon as you mouse over something it changes to something else and it will immediately change to something else and so on, and so on, unless you move your mouse away. So you have to actually rethink your relationship with the mouse immediately in order to read the book at all. And this is at a point where most people still haven't figured out how their mouse works, most people don't know what to do with their right mouse button.

CB: Well, the Internet requires a certain kind of technical competence, not just on the part of readers, but on the part of writers. A kind of technical competence which, I think, many poets would justifiably find intimidating. How are poets at Brick Books or Oberon Press going to write without their work becoming just an extinct species of emotional needlepoint? The poet nowadays must have competence in domains far beyond the rhetorical skills of versifying. Now they have to be typesetters and programmers; now they have to have an expertise in a variety of specialized vocabularies, be they critical or scientific, just to make use of a relevant lexicon without sounding completely obsolete or outdated.

DWH: Yes. But technologies are vocabularies, and there is an analogy to be made between poets who read other poetry and poets learning the technology that will allow them to write a poetry that remains relevant (or stands a chance of becoming relevant). There is a place for handicraft art—poetry included—because we have this bizarre cultural assumption that, although almost no one reads poetry, there is no other gesture that you can make that will expose your inner pain and the depths of profundity of your soul to the world, other than writing poetry, which is why people like Jewel and other celebrities do it. Despite the fact that they have no training in poetry and, at best, have probably read the Beats…

CB: But these biases constitute stultifying preconceptions that prevent people from actually knowing their language in a relatively intimate, profound way…

DWH: *laughs* That's precisely my point, that the preconceptions about poetry and the preconceptions about technology are similar. You learn how to write a relevant poetry and, at present, that includes learning something about typography and learning something about HTML and learning a little JavaScript, Perl, or PHP.

CB: Well, from a new technology to an older one: you've been pretending to work sporadically on a thesis about the typewriter…

  DWH laughs

CB: … and I'm wondering now what you think about the role of the typewriter, an old-fashioned instrument, and its effect upon poetry in this century.

DWH: Well, I believe that you can only really talk about a technology at the moment of its implosion, and we're just over the hill from the time that people wrote on typewriters in a serious way. Before my first computer, I had a Canon Typestar typewriter that had a little LED window, and it was this weird missing link between a real manual typewriter and a computer. So it's within our own lifetime that the typewriter has ceased being a useful tool.

My thesis from the beginning about the typewriter is that the typewriting machine proper, the operator of the machine, and the person who is dictating their wisdom to the machine and its operator constitute a kind of larger machine. And more often than not, the dictating voice isn't the voice of some sort of "other"—it doesn't have to be a real person. It can be a dictaphone, or an "inner voice"—the muse in technologized form. It can be the bugs in David Cronenberg's version of *Naked Lunch* transmitting messages from "Control" to the writer, or it can be Christopher Dewdney's alien intelligences that speak to the parasite inside the writer. This metaphor comes up over and over again, that the source of creativity comes from within the machine or from beyond the writer; it doesn't come from the writer. And the way that that assemblage, all of a sudden, begins to produce text in a kind of unprecedented emergent fashion fascinates me.

CB: Well, I think that one serious problem right now is that most poets in fact relate to a computer as if it were merely a glorified typewriter *laughs*, a machine that acts as an electronic substitute for the keyboard assemblage. We don't tend to produce books that can only be understood in relation to such computerization.

DWH: Yeah, I think that's very true. It's true from the compositional level all the way down to the telling details of typography. I'm sure that ninety percent of the people that are out there working on their computers now on their manuscripts are still typing two hyphens every time they need an em-dash and -- believe me -- it's a pain in the ass to get those things out when trying to convert that into a properly typeset book. But those kinds of details, like the details of syntax, betray a very deeply ingrained socialization about how you're supposed to relate to this machine, and, by extension, to language and culture. It's one thing to know that your computer can do all these wonderful non-linear things, but it's another thing to actually make it do them because it's easier to treat it like it's a typewriter.

CB: Well, there are models of efficiency already built into the device, features designed to extract as much productivity out of the user as possible with a minimum amount of effort. Your own work often attempts to misuse the device, deploying it in a manner counter to its intended function. I think that, ultimately, artists as creators must disrupt the tools given to them. And I think that, we have to think about the poet's relationship to the computer at the moment when the poet begins to realize that the computer is a televised medium that presents its own latitude of freedom, unconstrained by the recti-

linear grid of the typewriting carriage return.

DWH: So do you think that a book like *Eunoia*—a kind of inverse lipogram in five chapters, where each chapter exhausts nearly all of the words in English that use a single vowel—is a kind of monstrous text that pushes language and genre to their absolute limits? As a constraint, you're not piddling around with small potatoes there. You take language, which we assume, most of the time, is for communication, and turn it into this vertiginous other thing that makes you question every word that you read. And it changes the relationship of the reader to the text in a very strange way. It makes you incredibly conscious that every step you're taking is calculated, laid out in advance, is almost a kind of gnostic nightmare element to that, where you start to think of all language in that way. And whether or not you happen to be using any 'Es' in the sentence that you're speaking at the moment.

CB: Yeah, the text is truly nightmarish. *Eunoia* is a direct response to my own misgivings about the influence of Oulipo upon my work. The Oulipo is a French avant-garde movement that uses formalistic constraints to generate inspiration or innovation.

DWH: Misgivings?

CB: Oh yes, I can't swallow the aesthetic preconceptions of Oulipo without some critical analysis.

DWH: So it's almost a negative theology, in the sense that you're using the tool to question the tool.

CB: I guess. There's an element of critical experimentation at play in the book.

DWH: But I guess I'm wondering, does your playfulness reify the tool in the end or does it destroy it?

CB: *pauses Eunoia* is just an act of athleticism, a crushing endurance test. The word "eunoia" is the shortest word in English to contain all five vowels, and it means "beautiful thinking." I read through the dictionary five times to extract an extensive lexicon of univocal words containing only one of the five vowels. I could have automated this process, but I figured that learning the software to write a program would probably take just as long as the manual labour—so I simply got started on the project. I arranged the words into parts of speech (noun, verb, etc.); then I arranged these lists into topical categories (mineral, vegetal, etc.), so that I could determine what stories the vowels could tell. I then spent six years, working four or five hours every night after work, from about midnight on, piecing together a five-chapter novel in which each chapter exhausts this restricted lexicon—the first chapter using only words that contain A, the second chapter using only words that contain E, etc. I thought at first that the text would be minimally comprehensible, but grammatically correct and, as it turned out, there appeared these uncanny coincidences that induced intimations of paranoia. A kind of conspiracy was at play, I think, in the language, almost as if the words were destined to be arranged in this manner, that they lent themselves to no other task but this one.

DWH: Like the way that the vocabulary of Romanticism emerges in the letter 'I'.

CB: Yes, the letter 'I' was a strange chapter because much of the vocabulary was romantic or pastoral, and of course the letter 'I' in Romanticism is the privileged pronoun. The correlation between the content of the story and its vowel seems utterly uncanny.

DWH: Watching people who have not heard this when you read from it is really interesting because, initially, they're entertained by the rhythms and then they start to figure out what's going on and then they start to laugh, and then you keep going, and going, and going, and the laughter becomes a little strained. You detect a little edge creeping into the voice because they can't believe what you're doing and that you can continue to talk and you still have not exhausted the vocabulary of words that only use that vowel. The very real certainty that you have read the dictionary five times and found all of those words and used them, that's the scary thing because it's far beyond the limit of what people will allow themselves to think.

CB: That's why I say that the book is a stunt, Evil Knievel writing poetry.
DWH laughs

CB: I started thinking, "Geez, I can jump ten barrels. I bet that, if I just add one more, I can break my record." I upped the ante at every opportunity when I felt that I had mastered some component of the work. I made the exercise increasingly difficult. The univocal lipogram was not the only constraint. There were all kinds of constraints: internal rhyming, syntactical parallelism, even the number of letters in the words had to conform to a set of rules. It was a kind of fiendish crossword puzzle.

DWH: Have you had the constraint on constraint yet? Have you exhausted your interest in constraint or what happens next?

CB: Oh, definitely. I would never do this kind of project ever again. This book was an act of complete insanity. I could never summon up enough stamina to finish another work like it. I am going to have to shift gears and do something a lot more innovative and improvised, something more impulsive. The book has appealed to the worst aspects of my compulsive personality. I hope to incorporate more automated processes in my writing, letting machines do most of the labour. I think that my next work is going to be a long, nonsensical poem that looks lavish on the page, but, when read aloud sounds like a goofy videogame or a techno soundtrack. I need to do something more responsive to our late industrial milieu. What kind of writing do you foresee yourself doing?

DWH: Since I first got high-speed Internet access, I've spent an average of eight to ten hours a day online . . . that has resulted in a major shift in my thinking toward an interest in information flow and collective authoring. I think you can start to see it already in *the tapeworm foundry*. The work that interests me now demonstrates that the Internet itself is the poem—not merely a vehicle for poems. The Turnstile II project <www.stadiumweb.com/turnstile/index.html> generates "an endless ream of text by the live culling of network 'objects' from html pages, live chat,

email to telephone calls, faxes and incoming mail at Stadium"; Spamradio <www.spamradio.com> goes one better and broadcasts a live stream of voice-synthesized text from spam e-mails over top of cheesy techno beats. Bill Kennedy and I are working on a killer piece called "Apostrophe," which hijacks search engines to infinitely extend an old poem of Bill's . . . watch for it on my site <www.alienated.net>. And since September 11, after a series of long conversations about search engines with lucas mulder, I've spent five minutes each day collecting hundred of search-strings off of several major search engines. I'll stop on September 11, 2002. have no idea what I'm going to do with all that raw material yet—it's a Bruce Andrews-sized supply text—but I'm sure it'll be really fucking cool.

Okay, here's another *Eunoia* question—the finished book has been insanely popular by the standards of Canadian poetry; bookseller and historian Nicky Drumbolis told me the other day that he believes it's the fastest-selling book of poetry in Canadian history after Robert W. Service's *Songs of a Sourdough*. At the time that we were putting the final polish on this discussion, Coach House has reprinted the book five times, it's been reviewed in every major paper in the country and many places in the US, there's the strong possibility of a UK edition and you've just been shortlisted for the Griffin Poetry Prize . . . how do you reconcile its popularity with your avowed anti-populist stance?

CB: Well, I am very surprised by the popular response to the book, and I must admit that, while I am grateful for the attention, and even humbled by it, I do feel a bit sheepish about the success of the book. I wonder sometimes whether or not people are simply reading it because of its freakish character, passing by it like a carload of vacationers, slowing down to gawk at a two-headed calf by the side of the road. I am, of course, thrilled that people are enjoying the work, and I think that most avant-garde poetry in this country deserves much more popular support, so I hope that an encounter with my book might predispose the audience to look more favourably upon other more challenging work by some of our peers. I have no problem with poets acquiring a mass audience. I rail against poets who wilfully chase after such an audience by trying to write a work of popular appeal rather than by trying to write a work of radical excess. I think that artists cannot seek fame at any cost, but must earn it on their own terms, while making as few compromises as possible.

DWH: *Eunoia* is interesting as a counterpoint to your other major project of the last five years,

Ten Maps of Sardonic Wit, a ten-line anagrammatic poem made entirely out of Lego, by Christian Bök

the performance of Kurt Schwitters' *Ursonate*—the most complex and beautiful sound poem that's ever been written—because, in a sense, there's no record of that at all anymore, and that is something that I'm sure no one in this country has ever done, is learn the *Ursonate* from memory and produce a signature interpretation of it. And yet, I don't think that's something that you can even do anymore. I mean, it's vanished to the extent that you don't even do it.

CB: Yeah, I would have to take a few months off to relearn it. And I did that poem, too, as a stunt. I tried to teach myself sound poetry, but I didn't know a single sound poem, so I decided to start with the most difficult one—an act of bravado, I guess. I had to learn how to roll the letter R, for example, so I spent several weeks, standing in bus shelters beside little old ladies, growling *rrrrrr* under my breath. The fallout, of course, is that now I get to be a sound poet, probably one of the few my age, maintaining this kind of exemplary tradition in the country, even though sound poetry is only a minor aspect of my own aesthetic interest.

DWH: It's been enough that your performance, and that of other sound pieces, have, to a certain extent, kindled, if not a sound poetry renaissance, at least an interest in that work. But doesn't the whole sound poetry scene feel a little dated to you? Most of the people who do the work that we could identify as sound poetry—even major practitioners like Paul Dutton—have drifted over into the innovative music scene.

CB: Well, that's true. Most interest in Canadian sound poetry still focuses upon the practitioners from the early '70s. The people who admire bpNichol, for example, often reread him to the point of exhaustion, without finding a way to use such a predecessor as a springboard to something new in the same genre. I think that, because of this ancestral worship, we lack a large group of interesting, young sound poets. The avant-garde writers, our age, who do deserve some modest notoriety hardly ever receive adequate recognition by the mainstream, literary community: for example, the Kootenay School of Writers represent the contemporary cognate to the TISH Group, insofar as they are inspired by American poets, and yet, unlike the TISH group, whose members went on to subsequent fame in Canadian literature, enjoying academically recognized positions, most members of the Kootenay School tend to live in relative obscurity, and yet, their contribution to the history of experimental writing in Canada is, I think, more historically important.

DWH: I agree totally. But it's almost impossible to imagine having a school or a movement in contemporary culture without it being really precious or pretentious...

CB: Those notions of the school of avant-garde literature are absolutely necessary for consolidating moments in literary history...

DWH: Yeah, but it's just critical shorthand...

CB: Well, poets who don't fit within that critical shorthand don't get recognized, don't get an honoured place in literary history. Most poets nowadays have to enjoy an affiliation with some sort of collective endeavour in order to gain much fame for themselves. The same is not so true for novelists, because there, I think, a cult of personality is at play, and your fame, is assured through a kind of notoriety as a great story-telling individual.

DWH: A novel is still a commodity, it has some exchange value. You can't swing a dead cat in this country without hitting a First Novel prize or a writer that's won one. So, in that sense, being a novelist functions within the media culture quite comfortably. It's like that cartoon that Andrew Pyper has of the reader talking to the writer at the book signing saying, "I really, really enjoyed your hype." How many people buy the novel and then proceed to tuck it on to their bookshelf, unread?

CB: Well, they do so, because the book now is no longer a commodity to be read so much as it is a mode of cultural prestige. We do not buy books just to read them. We also buy books to demonstrate that, unlike other shoppers, we are "literate" consumers, making a small, but charitable, donation to our culture. No affluent citizen wants to appear uneducated about literature, so such a citizen might pay lip service to books in the same way that, say, Heather Reisman does when she opens her Indigo bookstores and then makes a big deal about supporting publishing in this country even as she proceeds to dismantle the very infrastructure necessary to sustain such an industry.

DWH: Maybe we all need to start packaging scented candles with our books. The best writing that I've seen about the Chapter/Indigo situation is on Brian Fawcett's website, Dooney's Café <www.dooneyscafe.com>. There are a number of articles there that argue that literary publishing is in trouble because superstores need to sell fungible goods to succeed. Books aren't fungible—you can't easily substitute one book for another and satisfy the customer. You need a large inventory of one or two copies of many different books to have a good bookstore, but you only need, like, three kinds of scented candles a season, and you can stock them in massive quantities, which is a cheaper proposition. And next year, when people want galvanized metal boxes, you buy them in quantity and lose the candles. You can't do that with poetry or literary fiction . . . unless you're Oprah, who's gone a long, long way toward creating a literary monoculture on the continent. And Chapters/Indigo clearly buys into that model, what with her "Heather's Book Club" radio spots over Christmas. Can't recall her mentioning any of her fave poetry titles, either. . . .

CB: There's no position lower on the totem pole of culture in this country than 'poet' or, maybe, 'playwright' *laughs*. For most people, poetry is the kind of artistic activity whose value remains completely unrecuperable, except as a mode of therapy, a quaint mode of self-expression that is completely interior and intimate. I mean, publishing a book of poetry is tantamount nowadays to publishing a diary.

DWH: But there's a certain crime in publishing a diary that's written in code. When a writer produces a book of poetry, people are automatically inclined to be sympathetic because they immediately translate that in their head as "this is a deep person who's trying to communicate their soul to me" and then they open it up and it's full of, say, crystals and references to obscure mathematicians and funny diagrams . . . it's not readily comprehensible in terms of the way that one is supposed to have structured one's soul.

CB: Well, there's little room now for critical contemplation of literature. A book is too slow for mass media. In a world where time is money, I don't think that books can compete. I don't think that any form of profound thought is going to compete unless it has the possibility of an extremely profitable outcome down the road. The disdain with which somebody like Mike Harris can greet a press like Coach House seems astonishing to me. The fact that a politician can hold his entire cultural heritage in contempt simply because it doesn't make money is itself utterly contemptible. Most of the great ideas in history have not necessarily resulted in immediate, productive benefits to anyone, and often such ideas actually demand that people change their utilitarian relationship to society. I think that many poets in this country have no interest whatsoever in the political mechanism of their own language. No interest whatsoever. I think that poets who lack such interest are like artisans who profess to respect their tools but nevertheless leave them to rust. What values are rewarded in this country? Not brilliance. Not innovation. We reward competent mediocrity, a quality that we admire because it represents an achievable norm that we can all realize within ourselves without having to change who we are.

DWH: Mass media demands stories that create a slight emotional disturbance but, in the end, restore a sense of the status quo—everything is right with the world. This is more of a problem with novels and film, but Steve McCaffery's poem "Teachable Texts" suggests that there are also moments where this applies to poetry. Even as quote-unquote avant-garde poets it's possible to capitulate to those kinds of pressures, to produce something that is avant-garde in a way that the academy can assimilate as a teachable text. So how does one continue to remain inimical to those kinds of pressures?

CB: Well, finding a way to live in the world comfortably without . . .

DWH: Losing your mind. A friend of mine from out west told me the other day that Andy Suknaski is living in a group home in northern Saskatchewan, medicated to the gills, not writing anymore. This is a poet who was fairly important to me when I was first starting to think about writing and, you know, just watching the pressures of being a poet simply tear the fabric of someone's life apart, not only ruining their ability to write but ruining their ability to live. It's like working with corrosive inks or toxic paint; language is simultaneously poison and cure.

CB: Well, I think that, in the States, you can't actually identify yourself as a poet on an income tax return. It's no longer a viable profession.

DWH: Yeah, but there's still hope. I mean, in Mexico now, if you're an artist you can actually pay your income tax with works of art. And the Mexican governmental collection has gotten so good because of this now, that artists are actually vying to give their best works to internal revenue because they want their work to be in this prestigious collection. You think, "Well, I owe them $40,000 or whatever, I'll crack out five paintings and that should take care of it." You know, at $8,000 a painting. . .

CB laughs

DWH: But people are giving them really good work and that strikes me as highly civilized. It's hard to imagine something like that in Mike Harris' or Ernie Eves' Ontario, but there is hope.

Not by Accident

SAMANTHA DUNN

I wake up in a hospital bed to find my leg swathed mummy-like in soft bandages, elevated above the level of my head, a series of tubes and needles lodged in the veins of both hands, a catheter tube taped awkwardly up my urethra. Dirt still crusts my scalp.

I am not thinking about pain because it is just there, everywhere, the world and the filter on the world. Next to my hand is a small device like a TV remote, but with only one button. When I click it a dose of morphine is administered directly into my bloodstream through one of the tubes running into the veins of my hands. A nurse must have explained this at some point; I don't think I knew it before. I quickly figure out that after a certain number of clicks the machine won't administer any more doses, even if the pain hasn't been beaten back. Click, click, click. And still it hurts.

I close my eyes. I open my eyes. I cannot say if an hour or a second is spent in between.

I become aware that Dr. Etmanon is in the blue-walled patient room. He has some information that is very important and detailed to tell me, and I believe he repeats this information many times, because I come to understand it.

"I need to explain some things to you: You have a barnyard open compound fracture of the tibia and fibula. This is a serious injury, Sam," he says. He's talking to me in a Zeus tone, as if throwing down thunder from Olympus. He doesn't look any older than I am. Younger, in fact. "Fractures are graded one through three, with three being the worst in terms of infection risk, soft tissue damage, and loss of blood supply to the area. You have a Grade III."

"Top of the class," I say, although the words said out loud don't contain the confidence of the voice in my head. My lips feel numb.

Dr. Etmanon refuses my banter. "Within the class there are groupings A, B, and C. Technically a Class C, a crushed limb, is worse than what you have because the bone is pulverized and veins exploded, but the severity of this injury increases exponentially simply because it was done by a hoof. That's why it's called a barnyard injury."

Barnyard, as in *bucolic*, as in *Rebecca of Sunnybrook Farm*. What am I thinking? I know better. My uncle was a rancher. My husband's grandfather, a share-cropper. I know about barnyards and all they represent, wading through the soup of mud and animal shit on rainy days, the sting of urine, the yellow bot eggs sticking to the hide on livestock, worms and other parasites. You don't even need a microscope. The barnyard has entered my body.

Dr. Etmanon is telling me the barnyard aspect is significant because it means the high risk of infection in this fracture has shot up drastically, further complicated by the fact that I lay in dirt and mud for more than an hour before the helicopter could reach me. He's explaining that this injury is messy, complicated. If I had been a soldier catching shrapnel it would have been better, because the heat from a bomb would have cauterized the metal. If I had been a biker in a wreck with concrete and steel, my bones in a spiral fracture like a green twig being twisted, even that would have been better because it would be cleaner. "That's why we have you on this IV containing a very aggressive combination of antibiotics," he adds.

The needles burn and ache because they are loaded with chemicals to blast infection. Heavy artillery. "At least there's that."

"The danger," he continues, stretching the word out, *day-n-ger*, "is that such a high dose over a week could cause the kidneys to shut down, and permanently damage them." He keeps looking at a clipboard, which is another weird detail that makes this seem like I am dreaming, because doctors from *Marcus Welby, M.D.* to *ER* have always looked down at clipboards in the exact same way. There are no emotions that haven't already been mined for sixty-minute segments on prime time. To see this gesture, and regard it as familiar, from someone who has just pronounced that my leg could gangrene and kidneys collapse confirms I have watched too much television.

Dr. Etmanon tells me that in the morning I will have another surgery that he calls a "debridement," during which the doctors, using powerful microscopes, will attempt to completely scour the injury for all dirt and sludge and fragments of bone, any particle of which will, if left behind, cause an infection that will take my leg.

"And possibly kill me in the process?" It is easy to talk about this because I feel as if this is a story I have seen played out before. It's an obvious plot twist, a way of revealing character.

"We are doing everything we can to make sure that doesn't happen," he says evenly.

"I'm sorry, doctor. You missed your cue." Morphine makes me feel as if I have been encased in cotton. "You were supposed to say 'of course not' or "that is out of the question.'"

"You lost a considerable amount of blood. The tissue damage is as serious as the bone damage in this injury," he replies. A plastic surgeon might be needed, because it could be necessary to take a graph from the latissimus dorsi, what in the gym they would call the lat muscle of my back, and use it to patch the calf. "But we will have to wait and see," he says. "I just want you to be prepared."

The good news just keeps coming.

My throat is raw from anaesthesia tubes; it feels as if I have had a tonsillectomy, and I start to wonder if they didn't make a mistake and take my tonsils out. But those are already out. Age ten. I had surgery in the morning and Mom brought me home at night when she got off her shift. She brought pistachio ice cream because it was her favourite and I liked it, too.

"I know this is difficult, Sam, but you have to know what's going on," he says. "The injury hit below the knee at about mid-shin, which means that circulation to the area is not ideal, it's a long way from the heart," he says, still looking down. "Because an artery was severed and so many veins cut, more than half of the blood supply to the area has been permanently destroyed."

"Irreparably."

"Sorry?" He pushes his glasses up higher on his nose.

"Irreparable. That sounds better than permanent. It's a question of word choice." I just want to sleep. "I worked at *Emergency Medical Services Magazine*. My mom was an operating room nurse for half my life. I know the drill."

I hit the button for morphine. The truth about a narcotic is that it doesn't take away pain or make anything easier, but it does extract from one the ability to care, to be concerned, to give a good goddamn.

The doctor is still talking. Because Harley's hoof was a dull, imprecise tool, the largest artery in the leg, which runs in the rear of the tibia, was damaged but not severed. The vascular surgeon was able to save it.

"If not . . ." Dr. Etmanon says, his voice trailing off into a kind of verbal shrug.

"If not, what?" I ask, wanting him to say the words, perversely wanting everything to be as explicit as possible.

"If not, there would be no chance to save your leg. We would definitely have to amputate."

To amputate.

Click, click.

Samantha Dunn, thirty-two, health and fitness editor, journalist, wife, book reader, equestrian, dog owner, recreational hiker, boxing-lesson taker, rock 'n' roll aficionado, blue-jean wearer, amputee.

"As it is," he says, "there is some chance you may keep the leg."

I look at him. He says this as if it were a known fact, but this information changes the entire underpinning of the situation. I thought we were talking about the chance of losing the leg, not the chance of keeping the leg. *The* leg, already not *my* leg. Something *other than, in addition to.* Now is the part where I would normally just turn and walk away from whomever or whatever presents anxiety, but I am weighed down by this *other than.* I have been hurt before but never like this. I realize I am hobbled.

> *And when I am formulated, sprawling on a pin,*
> *When I am pinned and wriggling on the wall . . .*

I was seventeen when I memorized that, an exchange student to Sydney, Australia. I thought I had discovered T. S. Eliot. *Have you read him? He's really good!* What did *I* know? In the tiny New Mexico towns where I grew up we had no bookstores, only a ragged library and racks of paperbacks at the supermarket.

Click, click, click. I close my eyes.

There appears to be a priest at my bedside, and this frightens me. Priests mean there is a death, or exorcism, imminent. My mother called the priest, like she called the priest the morning my stepfather died in the hospital. Frank got converted and had last rites in a sort of one-stop shop. No, the emer-gency room called the priest. The woman in the emergency room who wanted to know about insurance also had asked me at some point, "Religion?" "Catholic," I told her, but that was purely theoretical. If one were to have a religion, one would base it upon the mother and father's religious affiliation, and the socio-political context in which one was reared, factoring in, of course, the genetic predisposition toward papistry inherent in the Celts and the Italians, which largely constitute both sides of one's genetic history. It does not mean that since I had my leg ripped off I was expecting to see a priest. I don't even know how to say the rosary.

"Good afternoon, Samantha," he says. "God has given us a beautiful day."

Everyone in the hospital immediately calls me Samantha for some reason. Samantha is whom the phone solicitors and bill collectors ask for when they call, affording me the opportunity to reply *no hablo inglés.* If people know me they call me Sam, or in the case of some very close friends and some extended family, it ist Sammy—an interesting paradox there, that the most intimate friends and the most distant blood relation choose the same appellation.

His name is Father Fitz-something-something. Irish.

Butter on those boiled potatoes, Father?

Don't mind if I do, my child. God is great, let us thank him for the bounty he has given us.

The priest presses a blue-and-white plastic rosary into my grasp, and I am put strangely at ease by this act. The beads are round, smooth. The priest is also round, smooth. He is so very fat. Unbelievably so. His fingers cannot bend inward to touch his own palm. There would be no way he could move such girth without thoughtful consideration about where it will land. He has literally become the church, the embodiment of it, mammoth, with many folds.

"How are you doing, my dear?" he says.

"I must not be doing that well if they sent you," I say, but then again, I probably don't say that. My pillows keep sliding off the bed. Maybe I ask him for assistance with them. Assistance. Roadside. Things found along the way. Hitch-hiking once and a Nappa Auto Parts guy picked me up. Actually, my car had run out of gas on a strip of highway outside of Carlsbad that no one ever travelled. Snakeweed literally grew out of cracks in the asphalt. The fuel gauge on my Datsun never worked. The wipers didn't work on that car either, unless you pushed in the cigarette lighter. The heater made the headlights come on. The lesson is never buy a car from a man who wanted to take a crack at rewiring.

"I learned some serious voodoo driving that car."

"Excuse me, dear?" says the priest.

The Nappa Auto Parts guy was quite a stand-up man. Couldn't believe there was a nineteen-year-old girl by herself on that highway on the way to nowhere. Pentecostal, I recall. Part-time preacher. I love to hear those Pentecostals talk. Sexier by leagues than the boring born-again Baptists. Pentecostals are scary, because they see everything in life containing an element of danger. The sub-

text is always annihilation. Everything is forever about to end. There are signs everywhere. I always thought it made sense on an emotional level, but, practically, in terms of everyday life, they are all just nuttier than fruitcakes. *Nutty as a fruitcake.* Gram always said that too.

"Samantha?" The priest pulls the curtain that is supposed to act like a wall in this hospital room. He wants to offer me a blessing and this time I really do say, "Just give me the works, Father."

He places his hand lightly on my arm. The feather weight of his touch doesn't seem possible. Like something in a tutu. *Fantasia.* Elephants pirouette and poor little Mickey, how's he going to mop up all that water? I saw that movie with friends from elementary school in a matinee at an old theatre on the Santa Fe Plaza. We went to Swenson's for ice cream after that. Mom gave me money from her purse, which was a big tooled leather extravaganza containing lipsticks and used Kleenex and change, so much change it sounded like she was wearing sleighbells when she walked.

"Our Father," the priest begins, and I don't know the words so I just keep silent, as I did at the funeral mass for my stepfather. I sat next to Mom, on her knees on that wooden bench in front of the pew, her hands clasped together, her head bowed, her tears falling on the wood and I thought they would probably leave stains. They had been married for only four years. Tears: the steam that rises as the happily-ever-after evaporates.

The priest at the funeral gave the call and the rest of us the response. I read mine out of the paper pamphlet provided, but my mother kept her eyes shut and answered in a strange language. I tilted my head closer to her, watching her mouth form the words. She was answering in Latin. Holy shit, I thought. My mother hasn't prayed in church since Vatican II changed the mass to English. The act of her praying felt so private I turned my head away. How much I don't know about her. I cannot even guess.

". . . in your mercy, dear Lord," the priest is saying now, and it all seems so very beautiful that I start to cry. When I was a teenager I would ride my horse Gabe up to the top of Porkchop Hill; it was a mesa, really—steep sides and a level plateau—and once I was up there I would just sit and let him graze. The tiny tuffs of buffalo grass, when you look close enough, are perfectly formed arrangements. A Japanese design, the way the bluish green tone and pale yellow weave into each other. That made me cry too. And the delicate bones of my horse's leg, the slender cannon bone, the ball of the joint. All the strength and muscle come down to such fine sculpture. That also made me cry. I rode Gabe so much I came to believe my heartbeat was the sound of his hooves. I rode him until he was so tired his head hung like a dog's, and then I would get off and walk beside him. I swam with him in lakes. I would put my nose to his muzzle to breathe in the narcotic scent of alfalfa.

The priest is done with his official duty. That was fast. Nothing like mass. "Well, Samantha, you're in God's hands now. I'll be praying for you."

I move to touch his chubby hand and he lets me, his skin smooth and rubbery as a boiled egg. "Thank you, Father," I tell him.

After he leaves I finger the plastic rosary, and then I sleep, and in my sleep I know the words.

"Sammy? Sammy?" Matt's voice soft but insistent. Immediately I think there is something wrong. Something more wrong. He's sitting right near my bed and reaches to touch my fingers with his large, square hands. How is it possible that these large hands can weave sound out of six thin metal guitar strings? He would have been a natural blacksmith.

"Sammy?" he says again. Why does everyone keep saying my name? "I saw Harley. I went to the barn because I was so mad at him. I was going to kill him, but I couldn't."

I open my eyes. "What?"

He pets me in a calming motion, as if I might bolt. "I wanted to do something about you being hurt. I guess I wanted to take something out on him." His voice is reedy, as if it might crack. "But when I went there he was just standing in his pen with his head down. He looks so sad. It really seems like he knows he hurt you."

"I should never have gotten off," I say, wanting to clarify just who did what and why I am hurt. "I know better than that." This feeling is so awful. I can do nothing about anything. My world constricted to the size of a twin mattress. I start to cry again. More than I have ever cried in my life. I cannot wipe the tears away because the IV needles poke more deeply into my hands when I try to move.

People who don't ride always blame the horse, as if the horse is the one with the kind of brain that can build pyramids in the desert and create rockets that land on the moon. Matt used to ride with me when we were first dating. He hasn't done that in almost a decade. I haven't invited him, either. Did he not feel welcome at the stable, is that where it started to go wrong? Now he'll be the one to have to feed the horse, and he'll figure out how much money I spend on Harley and he won't believe it and he'll blame me; I'll be called a saboteur. He'll say, "We could buy a house on what you waste on this animal!" "We could afford a kid with what you spend here," or "I could buy five new guitars for what you waste on this animal, this murderous animal that could very well make you a peg leg, and who wants a wife like that?"

I wonder if I have been talking out loud, because Matt says, "Shh. Everything will be OK. Harely's fine. Drew and Janice are going to take good care of him."

I nod my head and turn the corners of my mouth up encouragingly but I am not convinced. Maybe the stable owners, Drew and Janice, will not want to take care of Harley. Maybe they too will blame him. Maybe everyone will decide that I shouldn't have a horse and will take him away from me, and I will be able to do exactly nothing about it. In the span of forty-eight hours I have become a child once more.

We sit with silence between us, focusing our attention on the television perched above the bed.

"Your mom's on the phone. She's wigged out." Matt holds the phone up toward the summit of pillows where my head lay.

"Please, can I talk to her in a little while? I just have to rest," I tell him. "Just let me close my eyes for a little bit."

Click.

It's likely Mom will call me a klutz, say, "Jesus H. Christ, Sam, what were you thinking?" or she'll laugh in that throaty, cigarette way of hers, and tell a story about one of my other accidents, opening with the line, "That reminds me of the time you . . ." She has many amusing tales in her repertoire. I am computing a mental list of all possible selections she could choose from, starting chronologically and limited only to those that resulted in bona fide physical injury requiring some level of medical attention, not just the bruises, or the scrapes and stumbles, or the near-misses. So far:

1. A split lip from falling on a wooden toy that had something to do with rabbits who ate carrots if you pulled them by a string.
2. A finger squashed by a car door when I was four and Mom's friend Natalie felt terrible about not checking to see that my fingers were out of the way.
3. An open wound on my thigh, I think it was my thigh or was it my back, from a bite when Smoky, a neighbour's guard dog, chased me down the street.
4. A broken wrist from riding a bike with a Barbie case attached to the handle bars. Mom insisted it was just a sprain until it turned purple and my grandmother said, "Oh good God, take her to the hospital, will you?" So we went in the back way and Mom's doctor

friend wrapped a fibreglass cast around it, which was great because I could go swimming with it.

5. A cracked rib and the sternum separated from my rib cage, due to a player head-butting my chest during a playground soccer game, in which the player in question turned out to be the son of a neurosurgeon my mother worked with, and I always thought she had a thing going with him because the doctors she knew, well, they were always unhappy with their wives.

6. A concussion, my first, caused when the saddle slipped underneath my galloping horse during a gymkhana for the Santa Fe Junior Horsemen's Association, in which we had been in the lead until the cinch—which I had hurriedly neglected to tie the knot on—came loose.

That's the list up to age eleven, I think.

"What, honey?" says a voice that sounds very much like my mother's, and I think, how can this be? Then I realize it indeed is my mother's. Evidently at some point Matt wedged the receiver between my shoulder and ear.

"My accidents," I croak into the receiver. "I was trying to remember the ones from when I was a kid."

"Uh hum. My poor baby. You better get some rest," which is what I say to her when she calls at two o'clock in the afternoon and has been drinking Scorsby scotch out of iced-tea tumblers.

"Do you know what a Grade III, Class B tib/fib fracture is? Is 'barnyard' a medical term?"

"Shit," she replies. She is quiet for a long time, or it could be that I fall sleep again.

"The doctor made it sound bad." I say.

"Shit." She makes that puffing sound which means she is lighting a cigarette. "You know the first thing I thought of when Matt called, don't you?" she says. She always asks questions as if she's setting up a punch line.

"Christopher Reeve?"

"Yep."

"I'm tired, Mom." My mouth is dry, and it feels like ants are marching all over my skin. The ants came all the way from that canyon in Malibu. How did the ants survive the helicopter ride? How did the ants survive the surgery? "There are ants, Mom."

"It just feels like that from the morphine. It's the way the drug plays on the nerves. There are no ants. Honey, listen to me, there are no ants."

I hear a sharp cry of pain that is not unlike the sound a dog makes if you should tromp on his paw. The room is now dark. The curtains, pulled. No one perches in the chair by my bedside and the phone is back in the cradle. There is another patient to the left of me in the bed by the door. We do not know each other's names but we do know each other's ailments: She is a hip replacement and a cancer of some sort; the cancer drugs made a honeycomb of her bones and her joint cracked from the pressure of her own weight as she lay in bed. She has three young children who cry when they come to see her, no husband, they will be orphaned on her death, but she tells them, Shh, babies, everything will be fine. She is experienced in true suffering, she bears it with a strength that seems to radiate across our shared room. Whatever she tells me, I accept as irrefutable.

"Pain pretty bad?" she asks.

The yelp was mine? "Sorry, I didn't mean to wake you."

"Couldn't sleep anyway. I need more drugs." She jams the call button for the nurse. "Morphine doesn't do anything after a while, for me at least. Ask them for Dilaudid. That'll fix you right up."

I would go to meetings with Matt while he was in drug rehab, and I recall the junkies pining longingly for Dilaudid. "Opiates," they would say with all the authority of a pharmacist, "are the fucking kings of all drugs," and they would return to sucking deeply on their cigarettes, nicotine the only drug allowed them in that expensive, Ambassador Suites_looking hospital. Experimental lab rats will happily hit the lever that feeds them the opiates until their lungs are paralyzed and they stop breathing. A rehab doctor said that during a lecture.

Click, click.

A wave of nausea. A side effect of opiates. The doctor had said that, too.

People are talking all around me but with my eyes shut I feel above them, separate from their concerns. "She's on an HMO. Which one? Kaiser?" "Did we get that transfer order from Kaiser?" "Ms. Dunn, we are just going to move you a little to your side," and "We're just going to proceed with

the schedule until Kaiser takes her." The last voice is Dr. Etmanon's. I open my eyes, which feels like exercise, a strenuous activity. "Sam," he says, slowly, "you're going into surgery."

He is bending over me. The tight furrows between his eyes turn the black arches of his brows into the shape of bat wings. "What does your mother call you?"

"Mohammed."

Name of the prophet. The Koran urges parents to teach children horseback riding, swimming, and good marksmanship. "Your family from Iran?"

"Good guess," he says.

"My mom and stepdad worked in the Middle East for a long time." I spent a summer in Saudi Arabia when I was seventeen, and saw a prince's stable where horses with bodies like greyhounds stood on marble floors the colour of snow.

He puts his hand briefly on my shoulder. "Mohammed?" I want to ask him if this is the surgery where they will take out my back muscle and put it on my leg, or if they could decide unilaterally just to prune, to hack, to cut off. But it takes too much effort.

Soon I am dreaming. I have the feeling of emerging from a cool, cavelike darkness into a bright, dry, California sun. I am on a trail that begins not far from my front door. I feel the impact of first one foot hitting the ground squarely, then the other. I can feel all the parts of my feet, the way my toes reflexively grab at the ground through the running shoes. My arms pump. My breath sounds loud to my ears. I keep running. I feel good.

An Interview with Charles Johnson

JENNIFER LEVASSEUR
& KEVIN RABALAIS

Born in Evanston, Illinois, on April 23, 1948, Charles Johnson's first artistic inclinations were as a cartoonist, but his pursuits have always been wide-ranging. In keeping with his earliest aspirations, he has published two cartoon collections, Black Humor *and* Half-Past Nation Time. *Other early interests, including martial arts and Eastern religion and philosophy, continue to enter his fiction and nonfiction. Johnson has also worked as a journalist and contributes regularly to various magazines. In 1970, he forged what would become a longtime relationship with PBS when he became the host of* Charlie's Pad *a fifty-two part series on cartooning. He recently contributed twelve original short stories to the PBS companion book* Africans in America. *Now, Johnson is studying Sanskrit.*

As a student, Johnson wrote six of what he now calls "apprentice" novels over a two-year period before meeting novelist and teacher John Gardner at Southern Illinois University. Gardner served as Johnson's mentor and helped him through his first published novel, Faith and the Good Thing, *which explores black folklore, humor, and magic. A story collection,* The Sorcerer's Apprentice, *and three novels followed.* Oxherding Tale, *which Johnson calls "a metaphysical slave narrative," tells a humorous and philosophically charged story of a mulatto slave. With* Middle Passage, *the story of Rutherford Calhoun's attempt to flee debt and marriage by stowing away on a ship sailing to transport slaves from Africa, Johnson became the first black male novelist since Ralph*

Ellison to win the National Book Award. Most recently, he published Dreamer, *a novel about the life of Martin Luther King Jr.*

Charles Johnson lives with his wife in Seattle, where he is the Pollock Professor of English at the University of Washington.

L/R: You've said that you knew your mother read the journal you kept as a child. In a sense, she was your first reader. Did that help you realize that there could be an audience?

CJ: I never thought about it that way. I guess she was my first reader. But she wanted to read me more than she wanted to read a literary document. After I realized she read it, I hid my journal. I would never think of sharing that with anybody, though I think my wife took a peek when we were first married. The intention when you write for others is entirely different than when you keep a journal. Sometimes when I go back and look at my journals, I see whole essays I've written. With a little editing, they could be excerpted and published. But most of the time, I'm trying, basically, to take my own temperature.

When I first started teaching at the University of Washington, I had my students turn in a writer's notebook twice in a ten-week period. I told them, "I don't care what you use it for, but let me recommend that you write character sketches. Maybe you'll see an image when looking out the window that strikes you. Write that down. Clip a newspaper article. Just show me that you're observing the world." Some of the students got so hooked that they didn't want to leave their journals with me over the weekend because they needed them.

Every writer needs something like that. I clip articles all the time, things that I think I can use later. They can be about anything: woolly mammoths, statistics about social life in America. A pile of journals over one foot long sits on my bookshelf. When I revise my work, I set six to eight hours aside to go through all of my journals and clippings, just to see if there's one thought I might have had twenty years ago that's useful, and very often there is. More than anything, it's a memory aid. The heart of writing is rewriting, revision. So the writer's notebook is critical; it helps me recall what I thought and felt about certain things. I think the purpose of a first draft of a novel or story should be written with the intention of seeing if you have something worth pursuing. You begin to clean up in the second draft. You take out what doesn't fit, and you fill the holes of the first draft. It's not until the third draft that you can really settle down and begin to revise. After that, you might go through twelve or twenty drafts to improve and refine. To me, that is not a lot to ask. Nothing is perfect. I'm not going to say certain things don't approach perfection, but the goal is to have something that is as consistent, coherent, and complete as you can make it in that moment. If you revise thoroughly, that moment might be a long moment. It might endure for decades as a work. Writing well is the same thing as thinking well.

L/R: You've talked a lot about what you refer to as your six "apprentice novels." Did you think of them in those terms when you wrote them?

CJ: I never intended to become a writer. All of my orientation from childhood to college was as a cartoonist. But then, one idea for a novel occurred to me, and I had to write it because it wouldn't leave me alone.

Setting out to write a novel was something I was familiar with because I had friends who were writers. One, Charles A. Gilpin, to whom I dedicated *Faith and the Good Thing*, wrote six books by the age of twenty-six, then died of a rare form of cancer. I wrote my first novel, and it was rough. I realized that I needed to know more. I started another one immediately to see if I could improve things like character and plot description. Then I wrote a third novel to see if I could improve structure. By the time I got to the seventh, I had read every writing handbook I could find. I understood a lot, but there were certain things I realized that I still didn't know. By good fortune, I happened to be at Southern Illinois University, where John Gardner taught English. According to editors who had looked at my work, I needed to learn two things: voice and rhythm. Those were two things that John was quite good at. He was a narrative ventriloquist when it came to voice. John paid an extraordinary amount of attention to rhythm, meter, and cadence. And he was also familiar with philosophical fiction, which was what I focused on for those six books that I couldn't nail.

L/R: So from the beginning, you have been motivated to write philosophical fiction. What made you want to focus on writing fiction in that way?

CJ: My background is in philosophy, and in that first book I tried to achieve the American philosophical novel, of which we don't have many examples. At that time there were about five or six people who worked in that vein, including Gardner, William H. Gass, Walker Percy, and Saul Bellow. This was a natural way for me to develop because as a graduate student in philosophy I read philosophers who wrote fiction—Camus, Sartre, Santayana. That is my little corner of the literary world. I've done other things because they interest me, but that is home base. The imagination is one thing, and that's fine, but if it isn't tempered with a base in the theory and practice of literature, then it's a wild imagination. That's not the kind of literature I'm most attracted to. I want literature to be intellectually vigorous. I want it to fit within the history, at least of the Western world, of the evolution of our literature. Why write? There's got to be a reason. Sartre writes about this in *What is Literature?* It contains wonderful chapters: "What is Writing?" "For Whom Does One Write?" "Why Write?" He says a writer writes because he has something to say that has not been said. That's why I write, and that's the kind of writing that I want to read. When I sit down to write, I think about what needs to be said.

Literature is like the sciences. There are objective problems in science that are handed down over generations, mistakes that were made, questions that were not resolved. It is the same with literature. There are books that need to be written. There are stories that need to be explored. There are subjects that never get treated. There may have been a book that treated a subject a hundred years ago, but botched it, making that book obsolete. If this is the case, we need to revisit that subject again. It's all about the evolution and the efflorescence of meaning and the exploration of possibilities. Most of our writers have not done that. This is an enormously complex world. They're eating cloned beef in Japan. We have technology that didn't exist twenty years ago. Some people compare the Internet to the Guttenberg Press. We are entering a period that will be as radically different as 1899 was to the 1920s, when we had a new science, a new poetry, a new evolving fiction and all the trappings of our world today did not exist. I suspect that the next ten to fifteen years will be just like that. It's a remarkable time to be alive. Some people say that everything has been written. Not so. We have entirely new situations. These stories are dying to see print.

L/R: How does writing historical fiction differ from writing about history? How related are these processes?

CJ: To write a novel, you have to know the history, and then you have to make up a story. I truly admire what historians do because fiction writers base what they do largely on that. But as a novelist, you have to know everything. When I tackled a figure as eminent as Martin Luther King, I had to learn many things about him. I didn't know, for instance, what his favorite sermon was, and it was important for me to learn that.

L/R: I didn't know that he smoked.

CJ: Many people never knew that because he never let the camera take a picture of him while he smoked, except once or twice. There's one picture of him where he's leaning forward at a bus station, talking to Andrew Young, and there's a cigarette in his hand. When he died, there was a cigarette in his hand and somebody took it out. He had gone out on the balcony to smoke, and that's when he got shot. As a writer, I need to know these things. One thing I couldn't discover was the brand of cigarettes he smoked. I needed to know the ordinary, everyday things. How did he shave? All of these things characterize an individual. Writers need to know all those details about a fictional character. For historical characters, it's great because the historians have already done all the work for you. But what you have to have is a story. History is made of stories. History and fiction are means of interpretation based upon narrative—beginning, middle and end—which, of course, is an artificial structure. You choose a piece of time that you want to work with. In that respect, the historians and the novelists are like brothers and sisters in their efforts.

L/R: Do you think fiction writers are able to enter history in a way that historians cannot?

CJ: One thing I like about *Africans in America*— which is the product of a ten-year project of historians working under the direction of Orlando Bagwell at WGBH—is that it is the first history book I've ever seen that has short stories in it. It would be great to see more historical books like this because fiction writers can get into the moment and sink the reader into it in a way that historians can't. I've talked to the historian Stephen Oates about this. I truly admire his *Let the Trumpet Sound*, which was one of my touchstone books for *Dreamer*. He said that he always wanted to go further with his book on King, but he felt that as a historian, one hand was tied behind his back. There were restraints he had that I didn't have. I could be speculative. I could connect things. One of the things I was delighted with about *Dreamer* was that I fig-

ured out what paper King was writing for a college course when he met Coretta. I could have her ask him what he's doing, what he's working on, and he could say, "Well, I'm working on this paper about..." There are a couple of episodes in *Dreamer* like this. King didn't have a religious conversion as a child. It was in Montgomery during a night when he couldn't sleep and was wondering if he should bail out of the movement that he heard God talking to him. King gives this event only three or four sentences in his writings, but I wanted to spend some time with it. There are possibilities grounded in the

historical record, but a historian might not reference these events and put them in larger contexts. One of the things I want to do as a novelist is look at all the pieces, come to some decision and connect things. It's all there if you want to do the work.

L/R: You wrote those first six apprentice novels over a two-year period. And then you met John Gardner. You've said that it was Gardner who taught you to slow down. How did he help change the way you wrote?

CJ: When I first started writing, I loved the work of Richard Wright, John A. Williams, and James Baldwin. They had distinctive visions. I hadn't gotten to my own vision yet, though I was trying to get there with a philosophical novel. One of the things that can seduce a young writer, unfortunately, is the publishing industry, which likes writers to turn over products very quickly. So a lot of writers produce rapidly, one book a year. One of the things I realized is how to deepen a work rather than just get it done.

It wasn't so much what John said. I'll talk about it this way: Gardner's idea was that you shouldn't go on with the next sentence until the last one is correct. You should not write below the best line you've ever written. He was a perfectionist in that way. He could sit and write for seventy-two-hour stretches. I've never seen anybody work that way. He was totally devoted to the craft of fiction. It was a religion for John. I think that's right. If you want to understand the craft, you must give total commitment. John would read my work and give me some comments, and I would say, "I'll go back and do that, but let me get to the end of the book first." He'd say, "You can't do that. You've got to get this part right now." I realized that I could get deeper into something with each draft, that revising is like filling a cup. Basically, what happens is that you fill the cup and it spills over. You add more layers, and things pop up in the fifteenth draft that you had never dreamed of when you first began. These things lead you forward, and the book grows out of its own potential rather than following an outline regardless of the other possibilities. This process also results in having to throw lots of pages away. For *Oxherding Tale*, I threw away 2400 pages to get 250. It was three thousand for *Middle Passage* and easily three thousand for *Dreamer*. There are issues I pursued that were fascinating, but they didn't belong in the book. If I hadn't pursued those issues, I would not have gotten to other things that do belong in the book. I keep all those drafts. There might be a paragraph or a line that might be useful in something else. There is a section in *Dreamer* where Chaym Smith shoots heroin. I wrote that scene in a novel back in the early '70s. When I was writing that scene for Chaym, I went back and found the passage so I wouldn't have to do the research again.

Sometimes there are nuggets of good writing that have to be cut when they don't fit, but some of it is publishable. There's a book called *Literary Outtakes* that includes poetry and passages from stories and novels that didn't make it into the final products. They are great, but they just didn't fit. The book contains a passage of *Oxherding Tale* in it. If you want a really good example of what I'm talking about, look at *Juneteenth*, Ralph Ellison's second novel, which was edited by John Callahan. There is a two-volume edition of *Juneteenth* that will soon be published that contains all two thousand pages of the novel. It will be very instructive for us to look at the complete, uncut manuscript. Callahan edited that down to 350 pages of a story, more or less, so we could have something after Ellison's death. In the 350-page edited version, we read that the main character receives a letter from a woman. Well, Ellison actually wrote the letter, and it takes up a whole chapter—and is probably magnificent in itself—but Callahan decided it didn't fit. Ellison probably would have decided the same thing. But you have to be open to every possibility.

L/R: How much does *Dreamer* differ from your original idea for the novel?

CJ: I worked on *Dreamer* for six years. The King stuff was easy. That was based on historical research. The hard part was writing about King's double. That was my original idea for the novel: suppose King had a double. It came from my notes. I tried it as a short story in the 1980s, and it didn't work. The double was tough. I tried him as an uneducated man who several of King's supporters had to bring up to speed, and that didn't work. Finally, through a series of co-incidences, I discovered who this guy was, who he had to be. I went to a black writers' conference in California. As I was leaving, the man who brought us there for the conference, Ricardo Quinones, gave me a copy of his critical book *The Changes of Cain*. I thought it was very timely because I was about to participate in a program with Bill Moyers on the story of Genesis. Quinones's book contains two thousand years of the Cain figure, from Genesis through Byron, where he is a reprehensible, devil figure, to his birth as the new anti-hero. If you want to know what I'm talking about, take a look at *Fight Club*. The film makes it clear that it is about Cain figures, men who have been rejected by their fathers and by God.

L/R: When did you decide to use the Cain figure as the double in *Dreamer*?

CJ: I didn't connect the dots until my agent called me after she saw the program. She said, "What about Cain as the double?" As soon as she said that, I found the structure I had searched for, the scaffolding that I had tried to discover for six years. I rewrote the book in about six months from that angle. The material became new to me; it was energized in a completely different way. It took me to a place I had never been, and that was exciting. Things take time to grow and become richer. I had to give it time. Sometimes, it's just luck. When I work on a novel for five or six years, my senses are open; I look for anything that relates to the book. When I was writing *Dreamer*, I asked myself, "How would Martin Luther King do this? What would he think about that?" That kind of dialogue was in my head all the time. It is an exhausting process, but I think it is the only way to create a truly rich work. Perhaps I picked that up from Gardner. I am sure I got that sense of devotion to the work as a gift from Gardner. There's something else I got from him that relates to this. He talked about moral fiction a lot. People sometimes misunderstood that. People often thought he meant moralistic fiction, and that's the opposite of what he wanted.

L/R: What did he mean by "moral fiction"?

CJ: John saw fiction, novels, in particular, as being a process. A scientist goes into the lab with a hypothesis. He says, "What will be the result if we do this?" At the end of the experiment, the original hypothesis may be confirmed or denied, or a whole new question may appear. According to John, it's the same with fiction. He liked to use Dostoyevsky as an example. Dostoyevsky thought to himself, "What if God does not exist. What would that allow us to do? Does it allow us to commit murder?" Dostoyevsky couldn't go out on the street and commit murder, but in fiction we have mimesis. He could create Raskolnikov and explore these questions without going through the actions himself.

My question in *Dreamer* was, "What if King had a double?" I didn't want to close off any possibilities. And by the end of the book, my idea about King and the civil rights movement was completely different than when I began the process. I now have new perceptions. In

Dreamer, as it turns out, Chaym never gets to be King's double. The long speech King gives in the church in Evanston, Illinois, was originally written for the double. Then I realized that he would not be able to do that. This is about Cain and Abel. This is about inequality on some basic level. So Chaym doesn't get a chance to be, in the full sense, a stand in. He and the narrator learn about King's life, and they are transformed by that.

As a writer, you may have a modification of your original idea, or the whole idea may go in a different direction. That is what Gardner meant by moral fiction. It's why you don't close off any ideas; and it's why you don't preach. Fiction is about discovery. It is trial and error, as in a scientific experiment. When you complete a project, you should be transformed.

Gardner said that when somebody writes a book and puts everything into it, including that person's best jokes and images, he is not ready to write another book for about two years. He needs to step back, live life, absorb the world. When I write a book, I write it as though it might be the last thing I ever do. I convince myself that this is it—my last will and testament in language. Gardner was big on the idea of emotional honesty. You need to go to those places that are emotionally difficult to visit, things that you don't want to confront, precisely because you don't want to confront them.

L/R: Did John Gardner offer you any advice as your work began to be published?

CJ: He said the real danger for a well-known writer is that you don't get edited; nobody touches your stuff. This can be very serious. He said that when you submit your manuscript, it has to be perfect. You can't expect an editor to work through every line, as Maxwell Perkins did. You have to do it all yourself before you send it in. But you still need a good copy editor and a good editor to ask questions like, "Don't we need a scene for that? Isn't this an idea you want to reinforce later in the book?" You need another eye, but you don't always get it. John taught me that I had to do much of that work myself.

L/R: In what other ways did he instruct you in your writing?

CJ: I was working on my seventh book when I met John. He was never my teacher in a classroom setting. I met with him in his office. He would give me suggestions about how to fix problems. I would usually go back and change the scene in a way that we hadn't talked about because I needed John, as an editor and friend, to identify the problem. That's the issue—the problem. I would find the solution. The solution has to come out of the writer's own sense of how this world works. John often told a story about a woman who approached him after a reading. She said, "I like your fiction, but I don't know if I like you." He said, "That's fine. That's the way it should be because I'm a better person when I write. I'm talking to you right now, and I can't revise what I say. But when I write, I can fix it." He believed he could fix language, even if it took twenty drafts, and make it more accurate so that it would not hurt anyone. And writing may be the only time in your life that you can be "right" because you can revise yourself.

L/R: You've put a lot of pressure on yourself to be a spokesman and innovator of black fiction. In the introduction to the Plume edition of *Oxherding Tale*, you wrote that you believed your level of success with the book would have an impact on more than just your writing, that the entire field of black literature could be opened if you achieved success. "Black fiction—as I imagined its intellectual possibilities—hung in the balance," you wrote.

CJ: I think that every black writer in America since the nineteenth century has been expected to write a certain way. Those expectations can smother the possibilities of creative expression. If you are writing only about racial oppression—and only about racial oppression in a particular way that, for example, white readers understand—you're missing something. Sartre said that if you're a black writer in America, you automatically know what your subject is: it has to be oppression. Maybe that was true in the period of segregation. But there was also Jean Toomer, who wrote *Cane* in 1923. He looked at everything, beginning with the nature of the self. It is not true that if you are a black writer in America that you automatically know what you are going to focus on, but there has always been that trap that black writers can fall into. Why is it that nobody paid attention to Zora Neale Hurston until the '60s and '70s? I'll tell you why. Richard Wright's *Native Son* and *Black Boy* are works of genius in the naturalistic tradition, and they defined black writing. He is the father of black literature. Hurston did not write about racial oppression. She wrote about relationships and culture. Her work was trapped in the background for a long time because of the conception of what black writing should be.

I knew when I began writing *Oxherding Tale* that this was going to be a danger. Some people couldn't conceive of black philosophical fiction, even though we have Toomer, Wright, and Ellison as examples. I was determined to make the things that interested me the focus of the book. It is a slave narrative. I did not want to deny the history of slavery, but this book is not merely about legal or political slavery. It's about other kinds of bondage: sexual, emotional, psychological, and metaphysical. The main character, Andrew Hawkins, has to work his way through all these types of bondage, some of which are even more fundamental than chattel slavery. Eastern philosophy was very useful to me in that exploration, as it is in all my books.

Writers, especially black writers, have to fight against limitations. One of my buddies, a Hollywood screenwriter, told me that all the stories that he is asked to write are black stories. But he can write about anything. Why shouldn't he be able to write about anything? It's about other issues. That kind of freedom is not given to black writers. You have to fight for it. You have to claim it.

L/R: In what ways do you feel that you have claimed your territory?

CJ: I'll tell you what I did with my editor when I was writing *Oxherding Tale*. He was a great editor, but he couldn't figure out the book. I gave him a ten-page, single-spaced outline. He wrestled with it. Midway though our conversation, I said, "I may not write this book. I think I might write a three-generation black family drama." His eyes lit up, and he said, "Yes. I can take that upstairs and sell it to the publisher right now." I went home and wrote him a long letter stating that I never intended to write that book. I wanted to see what he would say. And I knew what he was going to say. He was going to jump on that idea because everyone was excited about *Roots*, but that was not the book I wanted to write. I didn't want to feed an audience something that just reconfirmed its own assumptions and prejudices. There are other things I'm interested in. That is what *Being and Race* is basically about. It is about shaking up those presuppositions, not just through black literature, but through black American life itself. I think Ellison did a marvelous job of this in *Invisible Man*. We are mostly invisible to each other. One of the things that literature ought to be about is liberation of perception and consciousness. Our voices need to be freed so that we don't fall into those traps that diminish or limit other human lives.

L/R: It seems like you've actively tried to do this with each of your novels. Even when the character is a slave on a plantation, he's not the average slave we all think we know and understand. He usually breaks that mold by having an education and unexpected preoccupations.

CJ: Most people don't know anything about the history of slavery. They know a bit about Frederick Douglass, who was an incredible genius. And there are others like him, but Hollywood and literature give us images like the ones in *Gone With the Wind*. This is what *Africans in America* addresses. It clarifies the history of slavery. When I was in junior high school, we read no black literature. It was not part of the curriculum. I remember when my teacher in junior high school talked about slavery. She botched it. Slavery comprised a paragraph in our history book, and she passed right over it. I don't blame my teachers; their educations were flawed. They did not know about Harriet Tubman and Sojourner Truth, so they couldn't deliver it to us. Black studies started around the time that I went to college. The people teaching the courses were black graduate students in history and philosophy. I was pulled in with about twenty others to be discussion group leaders. I cut most of my classes that quarter because the discussion group that I led was so important to me. I got the idea for *Middle Passage* from one of the graduate students who was involved in the group. He showed us an image of a slave ship with little figures arranged spoon-fashion. That image burned itself in my mind. The next quarter, I wrote my research paper on the slave trade. That was the very beginning of *Middle Passage*, maybe about 1970. By 1971, I had written the first draft of the novel.

I don't fault my teachers for not knowing this history, but by now we should know it. I am shocked by how much general American history people don't know. For instance, the automatic stoplight was invented by Garrett Morgan, a black man. The phrase "the real McCoy" refers to a black man, Elijah McCoy, who invented the lubricating device for machinery. All this stuff is invisible, as Ellison would say. And then there are bigger things, as in all the black people who fought in the Revolutionary War for the crown and for the continental army. Most of that history is not known, and that's where we get assumptions, prejudices, and misinformation, which causes a lot of suffering. Literature can address some of that.

L/R: Certain areas of study, such as black studies and women's studies, originated to try to correct this lack of education. What are your thoughts on this type of categorization of subjects like history and literature?

CJ: These programs have the wrong approach. Black studies came about because the information was available no where else. It had to start somewhere. But I think the ideal thing to do is that if you're teaching a course in American naturalism, you present Theodore Dreiser as well as Richard Wright. A course on the modern novel and surrealism should include Ellison. Everything doesn't have to be Balkanized. That does disservice to the work itself. If black people are taken out of American history, nothing makes sense, not the Civil War, not the Southern economy, not reconstruction. History must be taught in a much more sophisticated way. So, again, this is the difficulty. All of our knowledge is provi-

sional; everything we know is partial. I believe that we know less than one percent of what is possible to know. Most of it is still a mystery. Knowledge evolves in physics, in chemistry, just as it evolves in literature. Whatever we think we know right now is subject to change tomorrow when new revelations occur.

L/R: You started with cartoons and journalism, then you went on to philosophy and fiction. Do you think your education and experience with these fields aids you as a novelist?

CJ: I don't rank the arts the way Hegel did, with philosophy at the top and music after that and then literature after that. The novel can be anything. It allows you to do things the short story cannot allow you to do. Students get hung up when they ask themselves, "How do I write a short story? How do I write an essay? How do I write a novel?" Don't worry about it. The engine of fiction is character. Everything comes out of the people. All you have to worry about is knowing who they are. This may involve research. You must know your characters and their situations. If you are faithful to how they would respond to things and you don't treat them as puppets to illustrate your own ideas, then you'll have revelations and you'll have a story or a novel. Readers want to know who these people are. Are these people I'm interested in? Do they relate to me? If they do, I must follow through with this because their stories may have implications for my own life. The hardest thing for writers is to get to the heart of a character, to create a character with more than one dimension, that is not just a prop that walks through the story.

L/R: You lived a long time with Martin Luther King for *Dreamer*. Where will you go from here?

CJ: I'm not ready to write another novel that involves heavy research. Maybe I'll choose something close to home, a topic that I already know something about, and that would take about two years. I'm talking to an editor about writing a book that would be like a *Souls of Black Folk* for the twenty-first century, something that looks at black consciousness in a philosophical way, but for a broad audience. It would cover the post-civil rights period. I've already covered much of that material in some of my books, so I'm not sure that I want to write a race book. I'll spend about two years on the next novel, which is sufficient if a lot of research isn't necessary. This is my year off to think about it and do other things. The Buddhist review *Tricycle* printed an article I wrote on Buddhism in black America. I truly enjoyed writing that piece. I think I've waited my whole life to write that article. When I'm working on a novel, there is not a lot of time for these other things. Everything has to be focused on the book and the subject. But when I'm not writing a novel, I can learn and do other things.

August Wilson recently gave me the three volumes of Borges's works: the collected short fiction, poetry, and nonfiction. A body of work is like a house. In one room, there are novels. In another room, there are short stories. In the next room, screenplays. The next floor contains drawings and comic strips. It's a round, diverse body of work. When an artist creates a body of work like this, it is all about interpreting this world we live in. There is a unity that is brought to that—whatever the subject may be—by the personality and vision of the artist.

The Ice Cracking at Dawn

CHARLES FORAN

My grandfather returned from the Second World War without his nose. He lost it in Belgium, and once lost, apparently, a nose isn't easily found. He served as an officer in the Canadian Army. On an inspection tour the bridge he happened to be crossing was blown up. A plank caught him in the face, making a mess.

As a child I was encouraged to touch the nose that surgeons rebuilt for my grandfather using skin from his buttocks. It was soft and wobbly and the slit-sized air holes were purely decorative. I found the nose repellent, but also interesting, like a cat stiffening by a curb. No cartilage in there, he would explain. Sock me one, and I won't even feel it. He also had a joke, repeated over and over: What an ass kisser this kid is. He'll make a great officer some day.

My grandfather's nose got left in the ground in Europe, a continent saturated in blood and guts and body parts. My father was only a boy in 1939, and only an adolescent in 1945, but he hasn't, I suspect, ever gotten over the fact that he never walked that terrain, a prospector searching a stream for rocks that glint. Had he gone to Europe, he would have understood more about a world where the bridge you were on might be blown up, and your features rearranged. He also might have understood, and perhaps liked, his own father more.

Instead, he grew up to be a man who met a bear in the bush. While still in his early twenties, anxious to put as many miles as he could between himself and his parent, my dad ran a mining camp in northern Ontario. One evening he was returning to the camp through the woods, using moonlight filtered through treetops as his guide. Tucked under his arm was a

.303, the barrel lowered. When something snuck up beside him and brushed the rifle, he nearly dropped it. He flinched at the stench and squinted at the outline. A black bear reared before him. My father staggered, and as he did he raised the barrel and squeezed the trigger. Because the bear was on its hind legs, it took the bullet in the face. Much of the animal's skull wound up in my father's hair and over his jacket. The next morning he returned to make sure the bear was dead. The corpse had settled into the earth, turning the soil crimson.

I was born in 1960 in a suburb of Toronto. I knew the dead bear as a bush story and the missing nose as a war story, and both were fragments, too vague and displaced to lodge as family lore. Though I could never have articulated it, I knew these tales came from worlds far away, where the ground beneath your feet ran with blood. I knew as well that where I lived was different. Where I lived, there was no ground beneath. Instead, there was television, and I grew up floating inside its dream, my feet in the air and my features glowing.

I like TV, and doubt it has damaged me much. I like the suburbs, and hold no grudge. I don't know who else feels how I do about growing up in the late 1960s and '70s, and I don't presume to be telling a story other than my own. That would be the story of my grandather's nose, and the son who was never given the chance to find it. Also, of my father's encounter with a bear, and the things he

may have wanted to tell his own boy about—the stink of a four-hundred-pound carcass, the taste of grilled bear meat—but could never find the right context, the right words.

And of that boy, golden with pixel glow, the soles of his feet as soft as a baby's cheeks. A boy staring at a screen and believing it not a mirror, or a portal, but rather simply a planet—his planet, his home.

As a shortcut, I could reconstruct a TV Guide from the era, run down the programs, the days and times, the repeats and specials, and make myself understood to some. *The Commander Tom Show*, every afternoon from 3:30 to 5 p.m., with *Gilligan's Island*, *Batman*, and *Superman* in rotation. Or game shows, in their morning-to-afternoon order: *The Price is Right*, *The $10,000 Pyramid*, *Joker's Wild*, *The Hollywood Squares*.

Or, by way of overkill, *The Brady Bunch*.

But I'd rather explain using an American rabbit and a Chinese philosopher. Bugs Buggy occupied pride of place in my childhood imagination. He was a smart, funny rabbit, and he could outwit any Daffy Duck or Elmer Fudd. *The Bugs Bunny/Road Runner Hour*, Saturdays at 5 p.m., was a religious observance, and later, when Saturday mass became an acceptable substitute for Sunday morning, I hung tough with the show. By then, I was maybe ten and knew all the cartoons line-for-line. I knew Bugs's great putdowns and I knew his mischievous good heart.

He spoke to me once. It happened in church. I was waiting in the pews with some other Grade Fives for altar-boy lessons. In front of us was the sacristy, the side-altar where the tabernacle, housing the bread and wine used during mass, is kept. Our church had a neat design feature—a hole carved into the low stucco ceiling above the sacristy. Down from the hole poured a steady stream of light that bathed the tabernacle in a saintly shaft, an implied revelation.

A friend dared me to look up the hole. I figured I'd see Jesus in there, his chest cracked open to reveal a meaty red heart, which we all kept breaking with our sins. I worried I might run into his dad, bearded and bug-eyed and wielding a stick. My knees buckled. I needed to pee.

It was lovely inside the sacristy light. Soft and smothering and more like sleep than wakefulness—the way watching television in the den on a Saturday morning, the snow falling outside and the rest of house still slumbering, could be. I knew at once I wouldn't meet anything scary. I knew it would be another nice experience in my nice life. The light did sting my eyes a bit, like a candle studied too long, but I squinted, rubbed them, squinted more. I saw smoke. I saw a blazing centre to the beam, a glare more powerful than any car hood at midday. *That* I could not look at, of course, being just a kid. *That* was God.

Then I saw Bugs. Inside the shaft, upside-down, in his standard pose—legs crossed, an elbow propping up his head. One ear floppy. Munching on a carrot. "Eh, what's up, Doc?" he asked.

The ancient Chinese philosopher Chuang-tzu was not a name I recognized until I was well into my twenties. But earlier, when I was maybe sixteen, I read a version of his famous butterfly parable. Chuang-tzu falls asleep by a stream and dreams he is a butterfly. On waking up, he wonders: Am I a man who has just dreamed he is a butterfly, or am I butterfly dreaming he is a man?

I didn't get the parable exactly—this was different from the ones taught to us at mass, like the story of the good Samaritan—but I knew it was about me. It was about staring out my basement bedroom window, watching nothing much happen on the street. It was about shooting baskets at dusk and cutting the lawn in the rain. It was about walking to school every day past other houses with basement windows and basketball nets in the driveways, and other teenage boys pushing lawnmowers over slick grass. The butterfly parable was about how my life *felt*, and I was happy to discover that some people, including Chinese philosophers, shared the feeling.

What exactly was that feeling? Of being alone, but not lonely. Of being solitary, but not isolated. Of never being sure if I was awake and dreaming or asleep and dreaming of being awake, and thinking that was okay.

So I watched television after school and on weekends, sometimes with my brother and sister, often by myself. So my grandfather died at age sixty-four, a man I barely knew, aside from the rubbery texture of his nose, because he was the father his son could never forgive. (And because they never walked the battlefields of Europe together?) So my father, once a bear killer, left for work in a suit and tie at seven in the morning and returned home at seven in the evening, and might watch

some TV later on, after the kids were in bed. So I might come out of my room, claiming I couldn't sleep, just to sit beside him on the couch. And sip his coffee, though it tasted awful. And pretend to smoke his pipe, though the bitter air pricked at my brain.

(Because he never took me hunting, and put me on a path with a black bear?)

In college I read the Russians. Of the major poets, Osip Mandelstam's lean, alert poems, had the greatest effect. "I hear, I hear the ice cracking at dawn," Mandelstam wrote in one lyric. Then there was the Stalin epigraph, which probably cost the poet his life. "We live, not feeling the land beneath us," Mandelstam declared. "Our speech inaudible ten steps away."

A bell rang in my head. There it was. The metaphor I needed to understand how I'd been shaped by a childhood inside TV. To live, not feeling the land beneath my feet. To awaken, never hearing the ice cracking outside. To not possess, in short, a relationship with my society, with my age. To not be alive, with everyone else, in a field of bloody soil and missing body parts!

Was there any other way to understand the world, and yourself? To understand your father, and so—again—yourself?

I have kids now, two daugthers. I am forty-one, and have still never gone into the bush with my dad. I called my parents on September 11, having just watched tower two of the World Trade Center collapse, on—what else?—television. They had done the same from their farm, where they had settled into retirement after leaving the suburb. We shared our horror and dismay, and then said it was good to hear one another's voices, to know that everyone was safe. My kids were asleep—where I live, it was evening when the terrorists attacked—otherwise I would have asked them to speak with their grandfather. He could have explained what had happened better than their own parent. He could have talked about hearing the ice crack at dawn and no longer feeling the land beneath your feet.

To my father, I should have said this: I don't miss the house I grew up in and I don't miss the basement where I watched TV. But I miss him, and have been lonely for him, on some strange, subterrain level, a current that I am only now registering in the soles of my feet, only now beginning to feel rise up into my body, an ache that might just be the ache of loss, all my life.

To my daughters, I should have said this: It was nice, how I was raised, awake inside my own dream. It was nice—everyone should be so lucky, really—and I'm even sorry it had to end.

An Anti-Sermon On The Mount

PICO IYER

Leonard Cohen's songs, a friend said recently, offer "music to die by," and as soon as I heard that, I realized one source of their Buddhist radiance. Death, loss, renunciation toll through every stanza of the benign hymns of passage on his latest record, *Ten New Songs*, and yet they're accepted, even embraced, as warmly as the love and life that have preceded them. When a poet of sixty-seven releases a new set of songs, it's a safe bet that they won't be about the classic pop themes of "Love, love me do," or "Baby, we were born to run," and indeed these new songs are all about the need for letting go. Cohen sings with the sober wisdom of one who's been living with death for quite a while now.

When the record begins—and this is more and more the case as Cohen gets on—one's first response is, likely, shock. His voice sounds as if it were emerging from the far side of the grave: a distant, muffled growl, as of a door slowly opening (or, in this case, more likely, a door creaking shut). The sound is spare, to the point of minimalism; the beat, even more than in early Cohen, is funereal. His croaks issue forth over a basic, leaden drone that sounds as if it was recorded (as in fact it was) in a friend's backyard late at night; much of the time, the singer's bass profundities are almost drowned out by the sweeter sounds of his colleague Sharon Robinson (her husband, Bob Metzger, is the only musician on the record, playing a faraway guitar). Whatever rock 'n' roll was intended to convey, I think, it was never meant to carry a sound as worn and old and rough as this.

Yet as you begin to settle into the very particular mood that develops—that of a cabin, high up on a chill mountaintop, in the dark, a single light on inside—you see that it is in the raggedness that the radiance can be found. There is a crack, as Cohen sings on another album (following Emerson), in everything, and that's how the light gets in. The opening song here, "My Secret Life," tells us, in effect, what to expect—for the secret life this singer confesses to is not one of venality and deceit and ambition, but the opposite. His secret, at this point in his life, is not that he's fallen, but that he occasionally manages to rise above it all. The mystic's way in every tradition is to invert the world by remaking the very terms with which it presents itself (turning its words upside down as a way to turn its values inside out); Cohen's secret life (since he's as impatient with the dogmas of the monastery as with those of the rest of the world) is the place where he makes love in his mind and refuses to see things in black and white.

As the songs go on, you see that, at some level, that's what they're all about. Babylon and Bethlehem—his favorite themes, his favorite places—but seen in a new light because Babylon looks different once you've been to Bethlehem. Cohen first met Joshu Sasaki-roshi roughly thirty years ago, and since then they've been drinking buddies, friends, and, in their maverick way, student and teacher. For much of the nineties Cohen actually went to live near Sasaki at his Rinzai Zen monastery in the high, dark, spartan hills behind Los Angeles, cleaning up, doing odd jobs, and cooking for the Zen master. He says (almost with pride) that he's come down from the mountaintop now—"I am what I am," announces one song, and another speaks of how certain "gifts" can't be exchanged (his gift, one assumes, being for worldliness)—and yet one feels that he would leave the monastery only once he was sure that the monastery would not entirely leave him. For much of this record it feels as if Mount Baldy Zen Center itself—or the meditation hall—is growling over the music.

The result is that we, too, have to let go, of all our easy assumptions and pieties. The second song, "A Thousand Kisses Deep," tells us again how the whole parade of human endeavour looks different if you see it in the light of death (or eternity: the terms hardly matter). We claim a small victory here and there, we think we've taken a step forward, and yet it all means very little in the face of our "invincible defeat." But, even as we move toward oblivion, we go back to "Boogie Street" (or Samsara, as it's usually called), and when we fall, we "slip / Into the Masterpiece." You can't renounce a desire until you've lived fully through it, and Cohen, who sometimes has the air of having entertained as many desires as a whole community of monks, has always been a believer in embracing everything fallen, the better to let go of it. As the opening line of the next song announces, "I fought against the bottle / But I had to do it drunk."

Cohen has long been one of the great realists among the romantics, never afraid to look at truth, however much it hurts. Indeed, part of his strength comes from the fact that he's always written so openly about his losing battles with women and intoxicants and the less exalted parts of himself. Here he brings that same merciless clarity to the very platitudes of the pop song. "I know that I'm forgiven," he sings later in the third song, "But I don't know how I know / I don't trust my inner feelings— / Inner feelings come and go." The next one opines, beatifically, "May everyone live," and then goes on to add, "And may everyone die. / Hello, my love, / And my love, Goodbye." In a sense, these are anti-pop songs, not least because they nearly all seem to end in emptiness, the void. And yet it is a nothingness that the singer manages to accept with calm.

The sound, as always, is sepulchral, and Cohen has always had an after-midnight quality to him (one reason why the reality of suffering pulses through him); however, in the earlier songs, one always felt that he was delivering his ragged, intimate confessions to someone else (a young woman, most likely, with a bottle nearby). Here it feels as if he is thoroughly alone, talking only to the dark. Lovers of the renegade adventurer will still find him kneeling at the feet of women, and talking of "getting fixed," but there's less of a sense here that these pleasures will lead to anything, or solve anything. Writing of death, he presents us with the least unsettled (the most composed) songs you could imagine; there's scarcely a trace of wistfulness or self-pity on the whole recording.

"The light came through the window," one song begins, and the singer, no doubt in his cabin on the mountain (where these songs were written), describes the motes of dust that are suddenly visible in the sunlight. Nothing could be more ephemeral, and yet—this is the heart of the whole record—nothing could be more beautiful. The world is an illusion, but it's the only world we have; you get through it by going through it, living "your life as if it's real." We throw our arms around the very things that flee from us. It's all the more moving coming from a writer who has over the decades written some of his most haunting songs about how beauty (and not its loss) can bring redemption.

Cohen was a leading poet in Canada before he ever recorded a song, of course, and he's long fit squarely into the classic devotional tradition (on his last record, *Field Commander Cohen*, among thanks to family and friends, he acknowledges his gratitude to Jelaluddin Rumi). When he writes a country-and-western ballad called "Coming Back to You," most of its power and resonance comes from the fact that you can't tell whether that's a "you" or a "You" (and, best of all, it doesn't really matter). Here, sitting in the dark alone—you can feel the confinements of time and space—he sings his most personal songs in honour of the impersonal; you hear traces of John Donne, say, or George Herbert, but often the small dark verses of power and compression sound most like Emily Dickinson—if she'd had a lifetime full of lovers to remember in her lonely room.

Part of the particular attraction of Zen for Cohen, one feels, is the fact that it offers a world outside all categories. No right, no wrong; no black and white. No life, no death, no Nirvana or Samsara. And one important aspect of this freedom is that there is no sense in which he has to conform to any standard dogma about what he should or shouldn't be doing. In his 1984 collection of psalms, *Book of Mercy*, he wrote a paragraph-long description of his teacher that is as clear and wiry a description of the Zen experience as any that I've read, and it ends with a classic Zen twist: "When he was certain that I was incapable of self-reform, he flung me across the fence of the Torah." It's no surprise, then, that many of the songs here sound as though they come out of the Bible, with their talk of Babylon (and even of the cross).

Yet, for all the open-endedness, *Ten New Songs* seems to me as unflinching and deep a record of the Buddhist experience as any I can remember encountering. Renunciation, after all, is only as strong as one's longing for what one is giving up (and one's never in doubt about the power of Cohen's desire); our sense of another order of things is only as meaningful as our understanding of the world around us. In his earlier songs, Cohen often almost shouted out his anger and restlessness in imagery of war that told us, over and over, that the world is a tough place, and violence is often called for; here there is a new tenderness that suggests that the beauty of the world lies partly in the fact that it doesn't last. One song explicitly sings about the dance between the "Nameless and the Name" (not what you usually encounter on Billboard's Top 40). Another talks about a couple "radiant beyond your widest measure."

That last line comes from the song "Alexandra Leaving," and of all the beautiful songs on the record, this is the one I can't get out of my head. Many of us, when young, read C. P. Cavafy, the great poet of exile, whose poems tell of his sense of sadness and loss when leaving Alexandria; here, a poet of a higher exile expresses his sense of gratitude and honour even as one Alexandra leaves him. In his younger days, Cohen almost defined himself as the man who left women in order to pursue his quest (the two most melodious songs on his first record were "So Long, Marianne" and "Hey, That's No Way to Say Goodbye"); now it is he who is left watching as love and life pass away.

As he watches Alexandra leave, he's tempted to find ways to cage the experience—to control his heart—by turning to his mind. He can say he just imagined the whole thing. He can tell himself he knew it was coming all along. He can say it was bound to happen. But over and over, he tells himself (referring to himself, typically, as "you") not to hide behind such strategies, or choose the "coward's" way of talking of "the cause and the effect." He has to take his loss as a man; more than that, he has to take it all as the greatest bounty he's likely to find. "Go firmly to the window," he tells himself, and "drink it in."

I listen to these songs in the dark autumn nights here in Japan and I feel as if I'm being taken as close to the unsayable as words can really take us. There's nothing passing in these songs (their language utterly transparent, their words so simple that they suggest many other words behind them), and yet things passing is their only theme. They give you nothing to hold onto—no specifics about time and place—and yet they go right to the heart. They're comfortable with mystery, you could say. Then the sun rises again outside my window and I see the brilliance of the autumn skies, even as the leaves turn and fall, and the chill and dark of winter draws a little closer—and I feel I'm hearing the songs being sung in a different key. Hello, my love, and my love, Goodbye.

BOOKTOUR COMIX # H2⁵ ··· Negotiating with the D͜e͜AD

MARGARET ATWOOD

Returning to Pakistan

KATHRYN KILGORE

I went to Pakistan twice as a journalist for several months in 1988 and 1990, travelling mostly through the north. I wrote about the dancing girls in the red light district of Lahore for the Wall Street Journal. *I lived in the nearly independent North West Frontier Province, under the protection of a local Afridi Pathan Malik, in his village, with the women, in purdah. Before that, I ended up one day in the Red Crescent Hospital ward in Peshawar, facing an eloquent and handsome fellow patient, Osama bin Laden.*

After September 11, all I wanted to do was go back to Pakistan again, and see how it felt now, from the other side.

I got the required letter from the Wall Street Journal *in order to secure my press visa to Pakistan. The letter said:*

> *November 26, 2001*
> *To whom it may concern: This letter will introduce you to Kathryn Kilgore,*
> *a freelance journalist on assignment for the* Wall Street Journal *in central and*
> *south Asia over the next several months, and perhaps longer. She has worked*
> *for us before and is a thoroughgoing professional. Please show her every courtesy.*

I packed, got everything in order, and went nowhere, because Daniel Pearl, the Wall Street Journal *South Asia bureau chief, was kidnapped in Karachi in January 2002 and beheaded soon afterwards. They did not show him every courtesy.*

I can't go back right now. Instead I am going back to the Pakistan of 1988. I could never write now what I wrote in 1988 because I no longer have clear access to many of the people I came to love in Pakistan, nor do I have their unqualified trust. And I am no longer naïve, I don't have that blind trust in myself, or in the innocence that allowed me to walk uninvited into any village in Pakistan, and into anyone's life, without fear, assuming my female, Western status, and my U.S. passport would save my life.

One night in July 1988, while Benazir Bhutto rode through Lahore campaigning for the Pakistan People's Party, I began talking to a Punjab police captain who wanted to practice his English. I was perched on a curb of the Mall, part of the Grand Trunk Highway, under the huge, over-arching peepal and neem trees. He was guarding a building on Bhutto's route from the airport, and he invited my friend and me to stand in the drive, and watch where we'd have some protection from the crowd.

We moved to the gate and watched 500,000 men pass (it may have been 1,500,000 men, depending on who was counting), following Bhutto's planned route into town. They paraded under the large green-and-red banners draped across the mall, riding on motorbikes, bus-tops, and tractors; riding on trucks. They waved PPP flags and chanted epithets about the president: "Zia fucks his sister," and "Zia is a dog."

"When a dog wants to die, he comes to the mosque (where he will be killed)," a fellow said, "and when Zia dissolved the government he was like the dog coming to the mosque."

And indeed he was soon killed.

Pakistan had a lot against Zia. His programs for the Islamization of the country aroused opposition especially among women who had no desire to be shoved back under veils and behind walls.

My new friend the police captain brought us tea. He said Benazir Bhutto was being delayed by this traffic. I mentioned that almost all the people in this crowd were men, and soon an entire group of Punjab policemen were looking for women.

When they found one, they'd point her out to me, and we'd all cheer.

A day later, as I walked alone towards the Anarkali bazaar, the police captain appeared with his officers. One of them said to me, "You cannot wear that scarf, it's a man's scarf, you must take it off and get a *dupatta*." The chivalrous captain said never mind. He handed me his own small handkerchief. He told them to leave me alone. It was a sunny morning, 116 degrees.

Late that afternoon, as I headed back to the hotel I came across the policemen again. They were sitting in the grass by the Mall eating mangoes. They were not in uniform and I didn't recognize them until the captain appeared. He handed me a slice of mango, then brought a jug of water so I could wash my hands. I asked where he had learned English. He said he was in school until eighth grade. He asked if he could walk with me towards my hotel, and practice English. I agreed, but then he walked ahead very fast, ignoring me, and would not speak.

When another group of police officers came out of the double gate of some official mansion and greeted the captain, he reverted to being gallant, friendly and entertaining. He stopped at the gate, stepped in, and beckoned to me. We sat in a huge green courtyard, and we talked about his village and his family. He was thirty years old. He made little money and could not believe that my roundtrip ticket to Pakistan cost $1200. I asked why he couldn't talk on the street. He borrowed my notebook and wrote, "because many people are like for every time laughing, but some people are not like for every time and laughing." I didn't get it.

Another policeman appeared, saying tea was ready. He invited us over to a small building. Inside, there was a table and a charpoy.

As soon as I saw the charpoy, I got it, what he wrote. By then, the captain was closing the door behind me. I told him to leave the door open; instead he grabbed me, and dragged me over onto the charpoy. I had time to feel furious and then afraid. Through an unglazed window I could see another policeman walking back and forth right outside, carrying a submachine gun, and I panicked, screamed, and kicked the captain. The captain sat up and rearranged his pants. He said, in a whisper, that my crying had hurt his heart.

One of his subordinates came in with a broom and began to sweep the floor. The captain leaned towards me, respectfully, shyly, and smiled. "How do you get to America," he asked.

I had come to Pakistan to write about women, and I was being taught.

On the PIA flight from Delhi to Lahore the pilot had said a prayer in Urdu over the loudspeaker, then added, "We will cross into Pakistan and land in approximately 45 minutes, *Inshallah.*" *Inshallah.*

Urdu, Pakistan's official language, is not everybody's language, and elections are not always elections, but Islam intrudes—or rather exists—everywhere, as an astounding moral force. My co-traveler and friend planned to collect data for her guide book, and I was going to collect stories on women in a Muslim country where the very borders are blurred. There is the disputed Kashmir-Jammu border with India. There are interior "Agencies," such as Gilgit, which in theory can join another country. There are enormous tribal "Areas" such as the North West Frontier Province, which are only partially government controlled, and where the police lay claim merely to the roadways and where guns are unregistered and common. There are twenty-four official languages, and forty-one unofficial languages. There were, in 1988, already 3.5 million Afghan refugees; some in tents, many in houses and villages that seemed to be permanent. There are Sunni Muslims, Shi'ite Muslims, Ismaili Muslims, Noor Bukashia Muslims, Sikhs, Christians, Zoroastrians and Kafir Kalash spirit worshippers, living among the ruins of Hindu temples and Buddhist *stuppas*. Animals wander around Bactrian Greek foundations, and a great many people claim descent from Alexander the Great.

Out of the plane, on first sight, there were no *burkhas*. The women just seemed to travel in packs. They wore bright pajama-like *shalwar kameezes*, as did we, and each had a large, sex-acceptable, *dupatta* draped elegantly over her head and shoulders in a casual, rakish style, that I thereafter practiced.

The men loitered in groups, talking, or sat cross-legged over tea. If they were devout, they stopped to pray wherever they were, when the haunting electronic voice on a loudspeaker called for them to face Mecca, five times a day. They watched us, while we tried not to watch them.

The Prophet Mohammad said to the men, *when you walk on the street, keep your eyes down and don't look on women.* To the women he said *when you go in public be in loose dress, cover your body and turn your face away.*

On the surface, these customs tended to work in my favour, however I could already feel that I was seen as a person beyond the law, and besides it became very difficult to interview any man with my eyes down, my face turned away.

Lahore is a beautiful city, an intricate park-filled knot of a city, with layers of history moulding in its architecture. We first checked into seedy Faletti's, then went out and walked for hours through the darkening streets full of men, looking, amazed, into the open bazaar stalls. The last few groups of women had disappeared with the last light. A man in one bookstall got upset when I placed a book with the word "Pakistan" in its title face down on the floor. "Do not desecrate the holy name of Pakistan," he ordered. Holy name? The word was made up right before partition in 1947, and is a blend of letters representing the five Islamic states that were trying to became a country.

It was on my first ride through the city the next day—as someone pointed out the Moghul fort, the ancient Anarkali bazaar, the old city gates, and Kipling's cannon—that I noticed the Bedford trucks.

These huge hauling trucks turn out to be Pakistan's lifeline. They are made in Karachi (their ancestors were made in England) and bought in the form of a stripped-down engine and chassis. Each new owner then designs, and has constructed, his own idea of a travelling work of art: his unique, high-walled, walnut-sided, tin-paneled, enameled (inside and out), portrait-and-landscape covered message, signed in symbols representing his origins, his hopes, his dreams, his loves, all reverent of

Allah; so that all this gilded, chain-hung, multi-colored finery becomes a moving prayer, designed to ward off the incredible danger of the roads. The trucks travel in packs, trekking north to China or north-west to the Khyber Pass and back down south to Karachi, their goods packed in poems and prayers.

I will play with you a game of love on one condition; if I win, I will get you and if I lose, I am yours, printed in Urdu, goes speeding by. The trucks are everywhere; as if their fleeting messages and images are needed to embody the real heart of Pakistan. As if they have to provide the only visual manifestation of the spirit of Islam.

If you overtake me, I don't care.

A side panel often carries a portrait of the driver's hometown, painted from a photograph. Romantic scenes are popular, as are animals, reptiles, ducks, eagles, and F-16's. A single wild duck means that the driver misses his friends. An eagle is the symbol of the national poet Iqbal, and also of the youngest generation; it expresses the sentiment that youths should be proud and should work hard for the nation.

The biggest symbol is always on the back, but it may be deconstructed if the truck is empty and the back panels are removed. The most traditional back has a portrait of the Taj Mahal, a tribute to the power of love, since the Taj Mahal was built by the Moghul emperor Jehangir for his beloved Nur Jehan. A truck might also have a political figure on the back—a faded portrait of President Ayub Khan, or a movie star, or a lotus flower, or a tiger, or a saint. A truck with the Khyber Gates on the back can only have come from the Pathan area near the Afghanistan-Pakistan route over the Khyber Pass.

Go with safety, come with safety, it says.

There are often eyes near the fenders—eyes with long feminine lashes. There are also eyelids over the headlights. The lines of chains on the front and the back of the trucks are hung with stars, diamonds, and hearts that nearly touch the ground and jingle loudly coming and going. They are like the chains women and animals wear around their ankles.

At the office of the Lahore-based daily newspaper, the *Nation*, I looked up the Women's Action Forum, which had started in 1981 and consisted mostly of upper and middle class educated women. They had published a statement calling for the resignation of Zia. Another statement opposed the Hudood Ordinance which contains instructions for the punishments for theft, drinking of alcohol, adultery, rape, prostitution, and bearing false testimony. The Ordinance makes *zina* (adultery) an offence against the state, unlike the previous British laws, which considered adultery a matter of personal offense against the husband. The law allows for public hangings, floggings, amputations of hands, and stoning to death.

Women are the trust of God in the hands of men, says the Koran.

In Lahore, I also had tea one day with Ahmed Rashid, a Pakistani journalist who worked for the *Independent* and the *Observer*, of London, and is also author of the recently published book, *Taliban*. Rashid looked streamlined by nerves, and he was on a deadline but he was generous, so he talked fast.

"Women are central to any political issue such as a change of government in Pakistan," he said. "The key issue . . . is the women's issue because Zia was impressed with the Saudi Arabian model of Islam. . . . During the period of colonialism the British created a secular Muslim elite, which is now the upper and middle class of Pakistan. So sometimes four generations of women [here] have been educated, whereas that's not so in Arabia. In Pakistan the elite is, and has long been, politically conscious. Women were involved in the movement against the British in 1947, for example, which won't fit into the Saudi Arabian mode. Also, the Family Laws are or were the only ones in the Arabic world.

"The support Zia had is from the new middle class, which was previously the lower middle class. They didn't grow up speaking English but they rule now. They are the military generals, the bureaucrats and businessmen who've been educated here through new money. The Jamatt-I-Islami and the fundamentalists get support from these people, not from the old elite, and Islam is the security blanket for the army and the new feudal class.

"Women in these societies, [in the] urban, educated classes, are the key. The key is in well-educated deeply rooted womanhood, which doesn't put up with this shit."

Rashid was expecting a call from London so he talked even faster. As I left him, he said, "If this time martial law comes, it's not going to be British-style. There'll be a lot of blood, a bloody coup, and one side will have to be wiped out."

I walked back to Faletti's, thinking of the stalls outside of the Wazir Khan Mosque deep in the old city, where they sell the curved ritual whipping knives, linked and chained together in bunches of seven, which Shi'ite men use to self-flagellate and thus purify themselves during Muharram. There are smaller knives for the boys. Pakistan felt frail, like its made-up name. It felt like it could get hurt, then return to being a poorer place, one with unsettling domestic problems, warring factions, provinces and religions; it felt like meat for an eagle.

In the meantime the black market was thriving. The huge heroin trade still followed the old route over the Khyber Pass and down to Karachi and on to Canada and the United States. The military had, in 1988, its billions in aid from the U.S. to fight the USSR, but some of that it spent amassing arms to threaten India. There were no government-sponsored social services in Pakistan, no help for widows or the old. The literacy rate had been stuck near twenty-six percent for years, and health was seriously neglected.

The military, by hook and by crook, ran the country, and controlled the civil service jobs, the foreign aid allocations and the nationalized companies, and planned never to give up its livelihood to any civilian politician, popular or not.

"If you want to know what a woman's lot is, this is it," Asma Jahangir said to me. She is a criminal lawyer, leading activist for women, children, and bonded laborers, and the Secretary General of the Human Rights Commission of Pakistan, and she is not talking about the upper classes. "A woman is always subordinate in the house, and from birth she is considered a liability. Some wives are divorced for giving birth to a girl baby, and generally friends will commiserate with a women who has a girl. Sons are then educated, and daughters are not. Among the poor, the male children work at outside jobs, and girl children work in the house. Girls are often married at thirteen or fourteen, although this is illegal. Polygamy is allowed if the local Union Council permits it. A man can arbitrarily divorce his wife in nine weeks. A woman has half the inheritance rights of a male, no divorce settlement, and widows get no money. A woman is the property of a man. If she withholds sex, a man can go to court and be given "restitution of his conjugal rights." There are no abortions, even for incest or rape. There is lots of domestic violence, among all classes. Lots of domestic violence. I'd say in ninety percent of families, there's domestic violence."

I borrowed a cigarette from Asma's desk, and smoked it.

Then on my way to dinner I visited the great, delicate, bony sculpture of the Fasting Siddharatha in the Lahore Museum. For six years he ate only an occasional sesame seed or grain of rice, and sits exactly as he has sat since the 1st quarter of the second century A.D., radiating peace.

Dinner was held on Tick-Tick Row, off Abbot Road. I arrived to the sound of frightened chickens squawking in cages next to fires and big woks. All the people eating, all the people walking along this row of stalls, all the beggars, all the teenagers, all the people lurking in the street were men. A male fellow-diner told me: "a woman would rather stay home with the children, feed them, keep them quiet, let them watch TV and sleep. They don't want to go out like men."

I watched the occasional trucks pass, bearing their messages, their expressions of passion, as I also watched the men lounging on the street, while I awaited my chicken. Tired and foreign, I didn't ask again about why the real women stay behind walls, while trucks are so lovingly displayed in public, with their long eyelashes, rhinestone jewelry and proud family histories; about why trucks are allowed to flirt, and to speak.

The prayer of a mother is the wind of heaven. These words flash by on the side of a truck as we exit Lahore and head northwest on the Grand Trunk Road, out of the pollution, past rice paddies and wheat fields and water buffalo, past nomads and cattle, sugarcane fields and bonded laborers chopping rocks, past the ubiquitous low ratty patches of marijuana weed. Further north, women are working in the fields with their faces uncovered. Then tents, camels, and brightly clothed Afghans appear in the hazy distance, their camps clustered in the low, dry hills. Fighter jets fly overhead. It is very hot, and very arid. When we later cross between Rawalpindi and Islamabad, there is a wall blocking the mess that was the U.S. munitions storage depot, before it was blown up. On the wall someone had scrawled "Our destination / Islamic revolution," . . . in English.

Pakistan borders (so the maps say) Iran, Afghanistan and China. It overlaps with India. It edges within miles of [what was in 1988] the Soviet Union. In defense terms it has no "strategic depth"; its roads, cities and factories are near its boundary lines. And it has Karachi, the only port in the region, and everyone wants it.

The northern landscape of Pakistan consists of tiny valleys, ripping fast rivers, and three major mountain ranges: the Himalayas, the Karakorams, and the Hindu Kush. The Karakorams are mad up-ended rocks swirled with lines of marble and burnt to a dry crusty brown. They radiate a temper tantrum of heat. "Relax, slide area ends," the signs say, just when you've forgotten about a landslide, earthquake, or glacial flood.

We head north towards anything wet and green, and towards the fabled Hunza (where people live forever), on the Karakoram Highway. Over two thousand people died building this highway, the only route to China. It follows the Indus, Gilgit, and Hunza rivers, running high on mountainsides following along the old Silk Route, and is 755 kilometers long from Takot to the Kunjurab Pass. The road took 20 years to build, with 25,000 Chinese and Pakistanis working on it every day. Riding on it, you can sometimes glimpse it winding far ahead of you, hung where there is not even a cliff to hang it on, way, way in the distance beyond your current hairpin turn, your current landslide. Even better, you can see it from across the valleys, a little light-gray thread far up there, winding north. So imagine driving this road in a top-heavy, loaded Bedford truck, and meeting another beauty going the other way. Praying helps.

Along the half-paved highway, rockslides come down littered with garnets. There are light green glacier streams and fourth century A.D. Buddhist petroglyphs carved on the big oxidized boulders by early Silk-Route travellers trekking from Balakot to Naran through the Babusar Pass to Shatiah and Chilas. There are still only a few routes people can take through these mountains, and so ancient paths have hardly changed.

We crept past Dards walking in the Kohistan area carrying their Kalashnikovs, using the mountainsides for target practice while waiting to make it home across the river in a hanging basket tied to a cable, and we found beds by the road as the sun set and mosquitoes rose. Our light bulb and fan quit at dusk, and too soon dawn broke to the sound of gunfire and the scent of kitchen fires. For breakfast I got a boiled egg, and when I cracked it open it had a whole chick in it, feathers and all. A message had come that our driver Ali's father had died in the night, and we had to get Ali to Gilgit right away—then find another driver.

Gilgit was filled with caravans of Bedford trucks, lined up and loading herbs and spices, cigarettes, dye, dried fruits, and whatever other unspeakable stuff to haul to China or over the Khyber Pass. The trucks were decorated for Eid with fresh black yak-tails, and the town was filled with polo horses. We bought food supplies and headed on north again with some of the trucks, to Karimabad and Gulmith in Hunza, the Ismaili Muslim territory ruled by the Agha Khan, and the most beautiful place on earth.

Hunza has nine mountains over 25,000 feet that you can see all at once. Until the Karakoram Highway came through, the local and only doctor told me, he had never seen or heard of a case of cancer. Thus the Hunza long-life fib took on another dimension, even as the really old men explained to me that their wives had done all the work, and that's why they had lived so long.

I could not figure out the legal status of Hunza, or why it was in Pakistan. The Ismaili women of Hunza have never been in purdah. There was a girl's high school in Karimabad, a women's welfare center, a maternity hospital, plus a feisty tradition of strong females. Some of this is thanks to the financial and spiritual support of the Agha Khan and his ancestors, with the help of the Mirs of Hunza.

How could this place exist? There are small Quaker-like green and white Ismaili mosques. In the blue unpolluted sky, the snow blowing off the slick top of Ultar II is so present that it hurts your teeth. The tiny fields and villages set in terraced steps above the sides of the Hunza river look like places one might like to live in forever; there are apricot and peach orchards, plum and mulberry trees, and dead gashop birds hang from sticks in gardens to ward off the plague. Somewhere, drums beat, after dark. What does this place have to do with Pakistan? What is Pakistan?

We went east, across the river from Hunza into the neighboring territory of Nagar. After the North and South Poles, Nagar has the most glaciers in the world, all of which meet at the base of

K2. Also, Nagar is Shi'ite territory; you don't see women anywhere, and the girl children are not allowed to go to school. Bibi Sultan, a retired school teacher in Hunza said about Nagar: "Our prophet said you must learn even if you have to go to China. Even the elderly should learn. And the Shi'ites are stupid to prevent their children from going to school. Religion is personal. Education is to walk with the world."

The men I talked to in Nagar were very serious, followers of Khomeini, anti-American. As one of them put it, "In my conscience, I hate you."

The rocks said *Vote for the stick*, or *Vote for the flower*, or *Vote for the paper hat*, campaigning to the illiterate.

Live like Ali, Die like Hussein was written on the back of a truck.

We left this dry moonscape of Nagar (a place stamped on maps in confusion as belonging to both Skardu and to Baltistan, and also just to "Northern Areas," and "Under Administration of Pakistan"), and turned back to Gilgit for supplies. There, another long line of fully packed trucks was waiting to start up the Karakorum for China. *Turn your neck and look /I have a wish /If you have a rocket /I have a truck*, was one driver's version of the hare and the tortoise story. I thought it meant "I'll carry anything." We bought enough food for several days and set off on a dotted line, the only direct road from Gilgit to Chitral. It goes over the Shandur Pass, where at 12,208 feet there is a polo field. This road, called the Punial Highway, is a dirt track that follows the Gilgit River, and runs in its beautiful, decayed way from sheer cliff-sides down through streambeds, and at best is one jeep wide. Every few years, the Pakistan Army polo team based in Gilgit and a crack team of ex-aristocrats, based far away high in the Hindu Kush in the former Kingdom of Chitral, ride for days bringing their horses up from their respective ends of this "highway," playing matches along the way, until they get to the top of the Shandur Pass, where the game was supposedly invented, and where they play killer high-altitude polo.

We passed migrating nomads with herds of goats and sheep, and people from far off villages carrying fodder and fuel home on their backs along this road, but no vehicles, because, as these people tried to signal to us, there was no road through. And so we came to a deep, fast river, with no bridge.

There was a council meeting of men from the local villages going on nearby, and when we appeared they looked at us, stunned. They had been waiting for months for the government to rebuild them a real bridge, but now here we *firenzies* were. So they went off and got their closely hoarded rare wood beams, built us a bridge, and took it apart as soon as we had crossed it, happy to see us leave.

Somewhere along on this road we passed the Agha Khan Burial Support Project, which seemed to be in charge of putting upside-down charpoys over gravesites; and further on we left the Karakorams and entered the Hindu Kush, with all of its passes to and from Afghanistan. Here we came into the Pathan tribal areas, where Kalashnikovs are as common as hats and clichés. We began to see hundreds, then thousands, of Afghan refugees. They wore their turbans in a rakish fashion and rode on the backs of Toyota trucks or on beautiful horses. A Toyota is worth two camels, and the Afghans have them both in quantity. Afghans in Pakistan do not farm. They build entire villages and keep all sorts of livestock, but food comes to them in Bedford trucks. In the town of Chitral, in the Agency of Chitral where we fetched up, there were ten Afghans for every three Pakistanis. The Afghans were selling dinner; great hot loaves of *naan* which they bake in clay ovens by the dusty roadside. They make ice-cream from glacier snow which they bring down every morning from the Nowary Pass. They pound tobacco and ash into *niswar*, a chewing plug which if fed to a snake will kill it in five minutes.

"By the grace of God you are very close to victory," said a sign on a young Afghan photographer's homemade box camera. The air was roasting hot. The next day we decided to take a break and go swimming. We drove north to find the natural hot springs up in Garam Chasma, ten miles from the so-called Afghanistan border. There, the sign on the gate to this "refugee camp" said, in English (which I heard no one speak), "It is illegal to take goats, sugar, food and other produce from Chitral over the border into Afghanistan." The village of Garam Chasma was what was called an Afghan guerrilla training camp, where the Pakistan military, backed by the U.S., gave the Afghan mujahudeen their basic training. The streets of the camp-town were filled with stacks of empty wooden crates that once held U.S. weapons. By the bread maker's shop a scrawl read, "be patient, and you will have victory."

There were no weapons in sight in Garam Chasma, following the Geneva Accord, but there were weapons here. The town was all men, many of them Afghan porters trying to get a paid gig to smuggle goods over the high pass into Afghanistan. Rakish young fighters rode in and out of the camp packed onto new Suzuki or Toyota trucks. The earth was all mudslide. The bread-makers were busy, as were the many tea stalls. Inside these low smoky stalls, rows and rows of photographs of dead mujahudeen covered the walls.

We swam in the abandoned scummy hot spring pond right by the derelict steam-bath shack with its sign that said: "Bath rooms under the Project/ Incentives to Poppy Growers In/Replacement of Poppy Cultivation."

Several months after our swim, the camp-town in Garam Chasma was blown up. It was blown off the map.

Going south, through the last Pakistan checkpost before Afghanistan, eight miles from Mir Kigani, and still in the Agency of Chitral, we entered a guerrilla controlled area and may have entered Afghanistan here without our knowledge let alone a visa. There were trucks along the road with no company names on their sides, which meant they belonged to the military. There were trucks with clocks on the front above their windscreens. There were trucks decorated with doves and with submarines. We paused at a mountainside tea-stall full of Pathan truck drivers, their long line of Bedfords parked with hoods open, cooling beneath a jagged line of pines. One parked truck had a sweet old-fashioned telephone painted on its side.

"A Pathan must have a gun and must have a few enemies," one truck driver told me. Right down the road we entered Dir, and the North West Frontier Province, the Pathan homeland in Pakistan. The houses looked like old movie forts, with mud and straw walls that are several feet thick and used to be bulletproof. Inside some of these forts are satellite TVs and Mercedes cars.

The Pathans live by three laws: *melmestia* (providing hospitality for strangers), *nanawati* (giving asylum to fugitives), and *badal* (an eye for an eye). *Badal* has gone out of favor. "The young generation doesn't like to fight," a Pathan gun-maker from Dara later told me. "Now we talk to our enemies, and our parents don't like it. Our parents say we spoil the whole thing."

Dir, the main town in the Dir Area, is called an "educated" tribal town, and it felt bad. The Pakistani police were there, carrying stun guns, and everyone else carried some version of a submachine gun. In the bazaar one medicine man was selling pretty red pellets. I held out my hand. "they will improve the sex life," he said, and the men around me laughed. Meantime our driver had disappeared. He wandered back later carrying a bag of dried opium flowers. "For my mother," he said. "It is used as medicine for the eyes."

We decided to rest up in Peshawar, the capital of the Afghanistan-Pakistan Pathan nation, before we went further south. In this incredible city of storytellers the language barrier began to lose its grip on my reality. Here, buses as well as trucks were beautifully cared for, decked out in colors and tin-stamped designs and signs (but not pictures),

watched over and polished by the river in the evening. The bus driver begins his day with the prayer, "Oh God please forgive me for everything." He has a radio and tape deck, and he plays the Holy Koran, and some religious songs before winding into the day-long blast of film songs. The bus is full of signs detailing the behavior expected of passengers. "When you enter the bus please say the name of Allah. No smoking: before smoking get permission from your neighbor. All parts of the body must remain in the bus. Don't be noisy. Co-operate with the driver and conductor. Children cannot have a seat, and must pay half fare. Throw dirty things outside the window, don't dirty the bus. If you ride on the roof you pay full fare—but you enjoy nature. Blow horn and take the way. Don't blow horn, you disturb the bus. Please ask God's forgiveness, this may be your last journey."

The road south from Peshawar to Dara Adam Khail is flat and picks up the hot wind from the southwest that kills all insects. It is lined with Pathan fortresses that dimly resemble a certain unfinished type of Spanish-colonial suburb in California. And no wonder. There are five hundred gun shops in Dara. Jeeps and pickups cruised down the dirt-lined and burro-crowded main street stopping to shop, and there was the nearly constant sound of rapid-fire weapons being tested. A rocket launcher cost $6,000, a stinger missile $10,000. We wandered into a large courtyard full of gun workshops, where men surrounded us, trying to demonstrate their pen guns. In an open stall a man sat filing away at an AKA. He ordered us sodas and passed us a Kalashnikov. "A Pathan is best with his rifle," he said, deadpan. "His pride is his rifle. Give him anything bigger, he'll mess it up." This man with his AKA began to take an interest in us and suddenly invited us to visit his village. Tribal, Pathan, kidnappers, I thought.

"There are more guns in the family than there are family members," he went on, adding that his small village consists of one tribe of thirty to forty houses, of families related to his father and his father's brothers. So we rode there with him. He left us in his truck when we arrived, and headed in to clear our way, and everything again became serious.

The house was fifty years old. There were stuffed deer heads and children's paintings on the walls, yellow flames painted over the doors. We sat in the main room while a long series of men came in from outside to shake our hands, and then sat down to watch us. Some of them farmed, some drove Bedford trucks, some made guns. Our Pathan host did not believe the Afghan war was anywhere near over.

After offering us glasses of spooky rose-water, he invited us to go into his mother's house and the women's quarters, pointing out the way. He, of course, stayed behind.

The mother was shy, pretty, and worn. Her daughters were all married but the youngest, who was thirteen. There were tiny pale babies lying around quietly, and aunts and neighbors and female cousins began to crowd in to tell us the story of the most recent big event: last winter's marriage of the second youngest daughter. She was fourteen and only too happy to open her marriage trunks, and empty everything out into our arms. She put on

her wedding earrings and headband; she put on her wedding clothes, folded for months, and showed us her thin, limpid infant. A cousin brought us a basket of bread and another took us to see the bed of the youngest couple, then the family refrigerator and the stable. There was a partridge in a cage, kept to absorb bad luck.

A young girl brought in a tray, and the mother handed us more pink rose-water drinks. An aunt appeared with a chicken under her arm and demonstrated that it was to be killed for us and cooked. We tried to play with some of the babies but they were not used to it.

We were led out of the family courtyard and down the lane, still inside the village walls, to the watchtower and the well, where we met many more women, carrying clay jars , the matriarchs of other households. They all shook our hands, and then so did their daughters and daughters-in-law. These women never leave this village, never. From one marriage or funeral to the next.

When we returned to the front courtyard, the men were still sitting there.

Our Pathan host talked about his grandfather who founded the village. The grandfather would not walk on the road because he hated the British so much, and they had built it. When Pakistan was created, a Muslim country, he still couldn't believe it. He would never use electricity, because that was also brought by the British.

Back in Lahore, we wrangled an invitation from a couple of shady male friends to go with them to the Heera Mundi, the "diamond market," with its famous dancing women. This is traditionally a place for men only.

The dancing girls mostly come from the class of families that have been in the business of prostitution and gambling for generations. A few families make a lot of money. Ninety percent of them are Shi'ites. In the Shia religion, if a man is out of town he can have a "mata" with a woman—a sort of casual short-term marriage.

The red light district seemed quiet and shabby, but full of idling male shadows. We were dropped off at a doorway, and climbed dark stairs to a small bright room, where musicians were warming up. We sat on pillows on the floor, our backs against the wall, and watched as six men came in and joined the small group of men already assembled. One was a famous poet, another was a famous politician, one of our pals whispered to me, and another was a famous filmmaker.

The dancing girls were beautiful. They talked with the men in a cheerful straightforward fashion as they strapped on enormous anklets of jingling bells. What surprised me was their clear eyes, their self confidence, their sister who hid in purdah behind a curtain, and their mother who sat in a corner and did not smile or even seem to move.

The politician leaned over and passed us about fifty strings of jasmine and roses, and motioned we should hand them, over time, to the two dancers. But that was nothing: the famous film-maker, who seemed drunk, gave us a huge stack of rupees, around $2,000 worth, in small paper bills, to throw at the dancers. "Like this," he said, and his rupees floated in the air over the young women's heads.

As the dancing girls began to sing and dance, starting out lively and fast, I heard in their songs and in the jingling rhythms of their ankle bracelets, the sound of a passing line of trucks crossing above the snowline on a jackknife pass. Under Islam "you may dress and make up for your husband but not for the public bazaar"—unless you're a truck, with winking eyes and long eyelashes peeking from under fenders. The Khyber Pass floated by on a lotus flower against a pure white background, with an eagle flying overhead. A movie star rested near an old Taj Mahal. Lakes, mountains, houses, trees. And "with the help of God and Mohammad, our truck will be safe."

A Tribute to Carol Shields

NINO RICCI

I first met Carol Shields in the fall of 1990. That was the year my own first novel came out, and as part of the promotional activities for the book my publisher had arranged for me to do a reading at a small bookstore in Winnipeg.

Now it just so happened—and it has since been my experience that there are many things of this sort that just so happen in that gauntlet of humiliation known as the Book Tour—that another reading had been scheduled in the city on the same evening as my own, featuring a writer much more famous than I was. I later heard that this other writer had attracted a crowd of some three hundred or so. But back at my own little bookstore, the appointed time arrived and what had seemed at first just the lingering end-of-day remnant of uncommitted browsers turned out in fact to be my audience— a total of six, as I remember, including the store's owner and my publisher's book rep. Among the rest,

however, were two people whose presence I had no right to expect: one was Sandra Birdsell and the other was Carol Shields. Coming from Toronto, I was not accustomed to seeing writers of stature attending the readings of two-bit first-time novelists. But there they were, mucking in like that to show a bit of support for the new kid. What struck me in Carol was the complete lack of any pity or embarrassment on my account for the poor showing— we're all here, her attitude seemed to say, so let's have a reading. In the end, rather than feeling sorry for myself for my meagre draw I felt sorry for the poor sod across town who hadn't managed to pull in Birdsell and Shields. That night still stands out for me now as one of the first times, with my intimate audience of six, that I felt myself to be a real writer, and also as a time when I understood what it might mean to be such a thing, to form part of a community that cared about words and took the trouble to support other people in their similar care.

Some two years passed before I saw Carol again, this time in the much different venue of the International Festival of Authors' Hospitality Suite. Any of you who have ever been near the Festival Hospitality Suite will know the strange, heady air that breathes out from the place, at once exhilarating and oppressive, the room so volatile with liquor and talent and ego you hardly dare to light a match. Somehow, in amongst all the luminaries packed into the room, Carol and I managed to come together at one point. There, amidst the flowing gin and the talk of New York agents and the drunken sixty-year-old poets pursuing young Harbourfront interns, Carol had the audacity to actually talk to me about writing, asking me, in her frank, down-to-earth way, how my own work was going. Again, living in Toronto, I was not accustomed to other writers ever making enquiries about one's work, much less listening if one dared to reply. But something in the directness of Carol's question and then in the unfaltering gaze she held me in, as if she wasn't anxiously waiting to move on to someone more important than me but actually expected, or more correctly demanded, a response, led me to set aside the usual evasion I tended to reserve for such questions and to offer an honest answer.

At the time I was well into the writing of my second novel and was encountering some serious problems of structure that had to do with trying to tell a story from the very beginning to the very end rather than starting *in medias res*, in the middle of things, the favoured method since Homer. We talked about the matter for a bit, and then Carol said something that floored me.

"Have you thought about starting over?" she asked, without a trace of irony.

No, I bloody well haven't, it was on my lips to say, thinking as I was about the years of work I'd already put into the thing and how I'd better get an-

other book out soon or everyone would forget about me. None of these concerns, of course, had much to do with writing; while Carol's question, in fact, had been very much to the point. She hadn't hesitated to ask the obvious, namely was I committed enough to my own work to put everything about it into question.

I finally stuttered some response to her along the lines of not being able to bear the thought of such a thing, which was more or less the truth. But afterwards I felt strangely honoured that she had taken me seriously enough to put such a question to me, and felt confirmed again in the sense that I stood before a true writer, who put the writing, and its voracious demands, first.

In our discussion, Carol had referred only in passing to her own project of the moment, which turned out to be a novel called *The Stone Diaries*. I read it when it came out and was at once reminded of the discussion we'd had in the Harbourfront Hospitality Suite—it was a book that solved brilliantly all those thorny problems of structure that I'd felt so daunted by, beginning at the very beginning and ending at the very end but still managing to capture, in that framework, not only the movement and drama of a life but more importantly the spirit of it, what seemed to remain when what was inessential was stripped away. And it did all this with a seeming casualness and ease that belied the novel's delicate layering of nuance and emotion and with no trace of the plodding inevitability to which many beginning-to-bitter-end narratives are prone.

There is no shortage of novels, of course—some of them great classics—that like *The Stone*

Diaries simply follow the lives of their protagonists from the cradle to the grave. A life, in fact, is in some ways the very model of narrative form: it has a beginning, a middle, and an end; every part in it tends to build toward the subsequent parts; and there is always a death in the final moments to bring an appropriate sense of closure. But novelistically, the recounting of a life in such a dogged, linear way poses certain often intractable problems. For instance, there is the problem of making the story sufficiently dramatic, so that you end up not with dull summaries of the endless series of events that make up a life but instead with a few select and vividly realized single moments, which must be illustrative of all that has been left out without seeming forcedly or artificially so. Then there is the problem of the connective links between these single moments, of imposing meaning, structure, and narrative drive on an entity, a human life, that often lacks such things, and again of doing so in a way that seems natural and inevitable, but not predictable. The virtue of beginning *in medias res* is that most of these problems are removed by virtue of having a plot: the Trojan War begins, rages, then ends; Odysseus sets out, has many adventures, arrives home. Within such boxes there is room for a hundred characters and themes and for a thousand flashbacks to whatever bits of background we need to make sense of things, all of this swept along by the rush of dramatic action. A life, on the other hand, has events, but generally no plot; it takes the art of the writer to sort one out, and to arrange things so that they seem to lead us in some sort of meaningful direction.

What struck me when I was reading *The Stone Diaries*, however, was how lightly it seemed to wear its cradle-to-grave structure, indeed using it as an opportunity for a playfulness and inventiveness that help give the book its peculiar air of buoyancy. More than that, it somehow managed to be a page-turner, though certainly not in the usual way of piling dramatic event on dramatic event, or of holding back some terrible secret which must at last be revealed, or of leading the protagonist along a trail of increasing dissipation or hubris that must inevitably lead to her demise. Rather, the novel seemed exactly to work against such conventions: the most dramatic event in the book is over by the end of the first chapter, and happens before the protagonist is even conscious; much of what happens to the protagonist afterwards is in the way of missed opportunities and small successes and not-quite-realized hopes that would have to be described, if they were told in simple summary, as decidedly unnovelistic. Along the way the protagonist has no overwhelming insights, makes no great contribution to civilization, commits no memorable act of humanity; and then finally she dies, slightly muddled and dissatisfied and embittered, and not at peace.

Of course, any life can be the stuff of a novel if it is well-told. But even in this, *The Stone Diaries* seems to defy the usual logic. Structurally the book is a dog's breakfast, a hodgepodge of recipes and letters and epigraphs and floating snippets of conversation and reflection, with a shifting point of view that, in defiance of contemporary fashion, is forever flitting from character to character, hardly ever alighting, in the end, on the consciousness of the main one,

Daisy Goodwill Flett. Then even in the more traditional narrative sequences there is almost nothing like the standard dark-and-stormy-night setting of scene and building of tension that is fiction's stock-in-trade. Instead, the most dramatic moments pass nearly unremarked, and many of the narrative passages are filled with the sort of introspection and editorial commentary that in a lesser writer would soon have fallen beneath the editor's red pencil. Indeed, the novel seems to break almost every rule that we writers traditionally trot out whenever we give writing workshops. Except that in the end it fulfils the only rule that really counts: it works.

What makes it work would be the stuff for a book at least as long as the novel itself. But even then we would be left inarticulate before the simple genius of the thing, the spirit that moves through it like the throb of our own unexpressed selves. Somehow it is exactly through its mess of broken rules and illegal devices, its mongrel heaping up of the flotsam of a life, that the novel seems to overleap those dilemmas I had felt stymied by, finding the elusive balance between the general and the particular, the summarized and the dramatized, the individual moments of tragedy and joy and fear that mark an existence and whatever it is that floats above them, and makes a life whole. It was this that most impressed me when I first read the novel and that still impresses me now, that sense in the book of seeing the entirety of a life spread before us, not artificially synthesized and made dramatic or instructive but kept in all its bumps and irregularities and indigestible fragments. And the magic of the book is how it still imbues such a life, despite its pettinesses and its disappointments, with its own beauty and mystery and grace.

When I first read *The Stone Diaries* I wanted to write a letter to Carol to tell her how moved I was by it, and how much I had learned from it. But the time passed and I did not write; and then the book was being so continuously showered with accolades that I hardly dared anymore to add my own little voice to the chorus. I regret now that I did not write that letter, and so am glad to have had this chance to redress, in part, that failure. I'm glad as well of the excuse this evening gave me to reread *The Stone Diaries*. What struck me in this recent reading was how much the book is about reinvention, about the possibility of reinvention, of one day turning a corner, or picking up a pen, or stepping on a train, and becoming new. And it seems to me that Carol's life is one that has been marked by her own ongoing reinvention, from academic to mother to poet to novelist to playwright to University Chancellor, and from someone doggedly working away for many years somewhat at the fringes of the Canadian literary establishment to Pulitzer Prize winner and international best-seller. But throughout it all she has remained what she first seemed to me when I met her: a true writer, someone who has stayed dedicated to her work through good times and bad, and who serves as a model to all of us in her unflagging commitment to the written word. It is that commitment that we celebrate tonight, for when most others would have been content to rest on their laurels and their legacy she has given us instead the gift of another book, for which we thank her.

I will die, in autumn, in Kashmir,
and the shadowed routine of each vein

will almost be news, the blood censored
for the Saffron Sun and the Times of Rain. . . .

   Yes, I remember it,
the day I'll die, I broadcast the crimson,

so long ago of that sky, its spread air,
its rushing dyes, and a piece of earth

bleeding, apart from the shore, as we went
on the day I'll die, past the guards, and he,

keeper of the world's last saffron, rowed me
on an island the size of a grave. On

two yards he rowed me into the sunset,
past all pain. On everyone's lips was news

of my death but only that beloved couplet,
broken, on his:

"If there is a paradise on earth
It is this, it is this, it is this."

     — Agha Shahid Ali
      from The Last Saffron

Errata

CECILY MOÖS

Lest our loyal readers think that all we do at *Brick* is publish timeless contributions to the international cultural discourse, allow me to delay this issue's embarassing enumeration of our countless mistakes in the last issue of *Brick* with a tale of love.

Indeed, through the efforts of our tireless staff, a foundering love affair was brought off the shoals of discontent and set sailing again on the seas of true passion. It all began with a letter, hand-delivered to our headquarteres, and redolent of fresh wax:

Dear Brick,
I'd like to purchase a *Brick* poster for my partner for a Valentines Day gift. The poster I'm interested in is a classic Canadiana scene with a man under a canoe—with a *Brick* in hand, and a moose in the background.
Signed,
MF

PS: My boyfriend, JH, loves your magazine and he writes about Canadian national parks.

You can only imagine how disquieting it was to think of our tender-hearted national-park-writer, perhaps on assignment looking into the problem of rope bridges, separated from his loved one and beset by squirrels and marmots. We set about turning up one of these posters and finally found one in a rare Canadian emphemera store, where we did not so much as hestitate before plunking down $1200 (plus GST) for the last remaining poster in existence. We then broke into MF's apartment, prepared a four-course meal, drew back the bedsheets, had the gentleman in question helicoptered down from the wilds and of course presented the good lady's love-object with the poster in a museum-quality frame. We stood back, beaming with pride as the two love-sick *amants* took in the scene:

Her: What the hell you doing in my apartment?
Brick: Please, don't let our presence prevent you from clasping each other to your respective bosoms!
Him: I've never seen this woman before in my life.
Her: Hey, you used up all my kale! What is this shit?
Brick: It is a vegetarian fricasee.
Her: Look, get out, or I'm calling the police.
Brick: Now, now, put down that andiron . . .
Him: It's funny, you know, I think my girlfriend lives in this building.

Ah! Spring is truly in the air. The rest of our lovers' evening will be available soon in *Brick: The Court Transcripts*.

Our Cupidity, however, won't distract us from our normal duties, which are, of course, our ceaseless lamentations over errors that make their way into each and every issue of *Brick*.

Let us start with the most egregious example. We took it on ourselves to use a photo without being sure of the credit therein. Well, we heard from the photographer alright, whose experience with *Brick* has clearly marked her in the most serious manner. She writes, "I sent the photo of the "Be civil to the shrine of poetry" sign from Du Fu's museum/garden in Chengdu, China . . . I am currently living and working in Beirut, Lebanon. Sincerely, Jennifer Mactaggart."

How these words chilled our blood at *Brick*. The consequences of our errors sometimes bring home to us in no uncertain terms just what kind of power we wield. What can we say? Come home, Jennifer! We are sorry! Armed with this very issue, show those so-called "friends" of yours that your dishonour is at an end.

On to a Mr. L. Scanlan of Kingston, Ontario: "I like the range of your literary journal, and though it's way too smart for me at times, *Brick* continues to grab me like no other magazine." We are glad Mr. Scanlan likes *Brick*, but we cannot say it to our readers often enough: regardless of your intelligence, you cannot let yourself be physically molested by a magazine. Our advice is simply to stand a safe distance from the magazine while in-store. (Unless you're into this sort of thing, in which case it would be courteous to withdraw to the poetry section for some privacy.)

Now on to the department of misspellings. We pride ourselves at *Brick* on putting most of the letters in the words we publish in their right order. When we fail with such parts of speech as verbs and nouns, we can breathe a sigh of relief that at least no personal harm is done. The same is not true when we misspell a person's name. To that end, we humbly apologize to Reza Baraheni, whose name we rendered in some manner other than the one he is used to.

Finally, it is with great pride that we announce the winner of last issue's "Translate That Caption Contest." For those of you who read our credits assiduously, you will have noticed that a cartoon on page 83 was not translated from the original tongue. The winning entry, by Luciano Pavarotti (no relation), is published below.

With great remorse,

Cecily Moos

Vo ist mein gepeck? Mein gepeck ist braun. Das ist nicht mein gepeck. Das gepeck hier ist rot. Vo ist mein gepeck?

The Usual Suspects

Mark Abley lives in Montreal. His book on threatened languages will appear early in 2003. Some days he walks around *gobdobdob*.

Agha Shahid Ali was born February 4 1949 in New Delhi, he died December 8 2001. He grew up in Kashmir. His last book was *Rooms Are Never Finished*, and his other books include *The Country Without a Post Office* and *The Beloved Witness*.

Margaret Atwood's comic strips appear regularly in *Brick*. She is also a writer.

Christian Bök is a poet and conceptual artist. His books are *Crystallography* (Coach House Press, 1994) and *Eunoia* (Coach House Books, 2002). He lives in Toronto.

A freelance journalist, **Samantha Dunn** is also the author of *Failing Paris*. She lives in Southern California.

Lydia Davis is the author of several works of fiction, including *Break It Down*, *The End of the Story*, and, most recently, *Samuel Johnson is Indignant: Stories*.

Geoff Dyer's books include *Paris Trance*, *But Beautiful*, and *Out of Sheer Rage*. A new book, *Yoga for*

People Who can't Be Bothered To Do It will be published next spring.

Charles Foran's most recent book is the novel *House on Fire*.

Carolyn Forché's most recent collection of poetry is *The Angel of History*, (HarperCollins, 1994). She teaches at George Mason University in Virginia.

Maggie Helwig is a Toronto-based writer. Her most recent book was a novel, *Where She Was Standing* (ECW Press). This essay will appear in *Real Bodies* (Oberon Press) in June 2002.

Fanny Howe's most recent novel was *Indivisible* (Semiotexte/MIT Press) and a collection of early short stories (*Economics*) is due out soon from Flood

Editions. Her *Selected Poems* was published by University of California Press last year.

Pico Iyer has been listening to Leonard Cohen since Richard Nixon was in the White House. The author, most recently, of *The Global Soul*, he has a new novel, on California, Islam and the dialogue between them—*Abandon*—out this winter.

Marni Jackson is the author of *The Mother Zone*, just reissued by Vintage Books. Her essay in this issue is from *Pain: The Fifth Vital Sign*, published this spring by Random House (Canada) and Crown (US). She lives in Toronto.

Kathryn Kilgore is a writer who lives in Key West, Florida, and New York City. Her articles, book reviews and poems have appeared in the *Village Voice*, *Montreal Gazette*, *Princeton Packet*, *Wall Street Journal*, *L.A. Times*, *The Nation* and many small poetry magazines.

Jennifer Levasseur and **Kevin Rabalais**'s interviews with novelists have appeared in *The Kenyon Review*, *The Missouri Review* and *Tin House*. They live in New Orleans.

Don McKay's most recent book is *Vis à Vis: Fieldnotes on Poetry* and *Wilderness*, published by Gaspereau Books, 2002. He lives in Victoria, BC.

Mary Meigs is a writer and artist. The drawings in this issue were created after a stroke left Ms. Meigs unable to draw with her right hand. She is retraining herself to draw with her left hand. She lives in Montreal.

Edith T. Mirante is the author of *Burmese Looking Glass: A Human Rights Adventure* and the forthcoming *Down the Rat Hole: Adventures on Burma's Remote Frontiers*. Her interviews with the Guam refugees can be read at www.projectmaje.org

Walter Murch is a film editor living in California. He is the editor of such films as *The Conversation*, *The English Patient*, and *Apocalypse Now Redux*. He is presently editing *K19: The Widowmaker* and has recently collected his translations of Curzio Malaparte. His discussion with Michael Ondaatje in this issue is from *The Conversations: Walter Murch and the Art of Editing Film*.

Nino Ricci's books include *Lives of the Saints*, and *In a Glass House*. His new book, *Testament*, appears with Doubleday Canada this spring. He lives in Toronto.

W. G. Sebald is the author of *The Emigrants*, *Vertigo*, and *Austerlitz*. He died in the fall of 2001.

Darren Wersher-Henry is a poet and editor. His books are *Nicholodeon* (Coach House Press, 1995) and *the tapeworm foundry* (House of Anansi Press, 2000).

James Wood is senior editor at the New Republic, and an eminent literary critic and writer. He is the author of *The Broken Estate, Essays on Literature and Belief*.

Credits

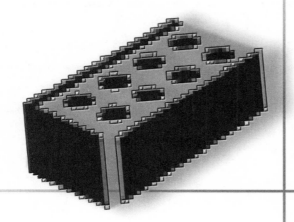

{Brickus Magazinus}

{Pages Bookstorius}

{Original contemporary literature found here.}

Pages Books & Magazines • 256 Queen Street West, Toronto ON M5V 1Z8 • (voice) 416•598•1447 (fax) 416•598•2042

THE GRIFFIN POETRY PRIZE

THE GRIFFIN TRUST FOR EXCELLENCE IN POETRY

ANNOUNCES
SHORTLISTED BOOKS FOR 2002

CANADIAN PRIZE $40,000

Eunoia • **Christian Bök**
Coach House Books

Sheep's Vigil by a Fervent Person • **Eirin Moure**
House of Anansi Press

Short Haul Engine • **Karen Solie**
Brick Books

INTERNATIONAL PRIZE $40,000

Maraca New and Selected Poems 1965-2000 • **Victor Hernández Cruz**
Coffee House Press

Homer: War Music • **Christopher Logue**
Faber and Faber Limited

Conscious and Verbal • **Les Murray**
Farrar, Straus & Giroux

Disobedience • **Alice Notley**
Penguin Putnam Inc.

Shortlist Readings at Harbourfront on May 29th • Awards Ceremony, May 30th
Telephone (905) 565-5993 www.griffinpoetryprize.com

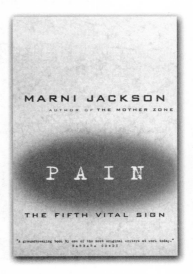

Humber School for Writers Summer Workshop

July 20 – July 26

Featuring: Stevie Cameron, Wayson Choy, Bruce Jay Friedman, Isabel Huggan, John Metcalf, Kim Moritsugu, Tim O'Brien, Paul Quarrington, Nino Ricci, Robert Sawyer, Richard Scrimger, Olive Senior, D. M. Thomas

For more information, call 416.675.5084

Humber College, Toronto, Ontario, Canada

Why don't you invite us in?

Brick can come right to your house, if you tell us where you live*

Please send me two years (four issues) of BRICK. I'm including:

○ $38 for Canada ○ US$41 for the States ○ US$46 elsewhere
(including GST)

Name
_____

Address
_____

_____

Email
_____

Nobody who cares about books or life could be disappointed in Brick. — Alice Munro

---

Brick is the gift that keeps on giving.

(Well, for two years at least.)

Please send someone I like two years (four issues) of BRICK. I'm including:

○ $38 for Canada ○ US$41 for the States ○ US$46 elsewhere
(including GST)

Name
_____

Address
_____

_____

Email
_____

Your name
_____

Brick is one of the best journals of ideas published in the English-speaking world. — Russell Banks

PLEASE INCLUDE THIS CARD WITH
YOUR PAYMENT AND MAIL TO:

BRICK

BOX 537, STN Q.

TORONTO, ONTARIO

M4T 2M5 CANADA

PLEASE INCLUDE THIS CARD WITH
YOUR PAYMENT AND MAIL TO:

BRICK

BOX 537, STN Q.

TORONTO, ONTARIO

M4T 2M5 CANADA